TABLE OF CONTENTS

THE PROCRAS TINATION LOOP

Stop Overthinking and Postponing.
Get Things Done by Building Good Habits.
Increase Your Productivity!

LEO CHU

INTRODUCTION

Let's be honest: you didn't seek out a book on procrastination because your task list is blank and you've got nothing but time to burn. You're reading this because you feel things aren't getting done. Or they are—but only at the eleventh hour, and always with your blood pressure somewhere near orbit.

Perhaps, you've fallen into the habit of staring at whatever task is at hand like it's some feral animal. You circle it. You Google how to do it. You make a playlist to do it. You tidy up your desk and lay out your work station in preparation. And the next thing you know… it's 2:14 a.m. and you're on your fifth YouTube video.

Welcome to the Procrastination Loop.

Here's the truth: Procrastination, at least way more often than not, is just *fear dressed up as perfectionism*. Or emotional fatigue disguised in a productivity costume. Overthinking, on the other hand, is just your brain trying to "logic" its way around uncomfortable action. It's a smart counter-tactic by your brain, but it's certainly not helpful for you.

This book is your way out.

In the pages ahead, we're going to dissect that loop. We're going to do so cleanly, painlessly, and, just as importantly, *with no shame*. We'll uncover *what causes it*, *why your brain cooperates with it*, and most importantly, *how to break it*. You'll learn how to *reset your thoughts*, *manage your energy* (and not just your time), and *build simple, sustainable habits that actually stick*. I haven't written this book to be a motivational speech in book form. There are enough of those in circulation. I've written it to be as comprehensive a toolbox for eliminating procrastination as you're ever likely to find.

I'll talk to you like a friend, all through. You'll get zero fluff and 100% clarity. You'll find reasonably short chapters that are packed with substance, tangible next steps, and small wins that should quickly add up. And in the event that you think your focus has been thoroughly fried by thousands of hours of social media scrolls—worry not.

I have written this book for *real people with real issues and real distractions*.

If you've been looking for something that would finally enable you to get follow-through on the things *you know matter most*, then you've found it. If you have big goals but low motivation, this is THE guidebook for you. If your brain is bloated with "shoulds," "somedays," and "maybe laters," we're going to sort all of that out.

The loop stops here.

Let's get started.

But before that, and to thank you to have purchased this book, here is your gift:

SECTION 1

UNDERSTANDING THE INNER MECHANICS OF PROCRASTINATION

To fully understand procrastination and be able to deal with and overcome it, we must first understand what's really happening beneath the surface. But before we cover that, let's first understand procrastination and how it is closely linked to overthinking – including how there is a loop that keeps both feeding into each other.

CHAPTER 1

WHAT IS PROCRASTINATION AND OVERTHINKING, REALLY?

The first chapter of this section is aimed at helping you completely understand procrastination, overthinking, and how both of these feed into each other, so that you are better placed to break the habit for good. We'll unpack every descriptive and foundational aspect you need to know about in simple, clear, cohesive and comprehensive detail.

Let's get to it.

What Exactly Is Procrastination (The Act of Avoiding)

Procrastination is *the intentional delay of a task despite knowing that doing so will have a negative impact*. You know the deadline is approaching. You know that putting it off will make you stressed. You know that it will perhaps even spoil the outcome. And yet—you delay.

As such, two elements combine to make procrastination what it is: intentional delay and awareness of the costs of doing so. It's not that you "forgot" or didn't have time. It's that you knew what you were delaying, knew what it might cost you… and yet did it anyway.

Now, it's important to differentiate procrastination from something more intentional: prioritization. Choosing to delay a task because something more significant or time-sensitive needs your attention? That's *time management*, which is far removed from procrastination. Similarly, taking a break from a task to recharge and come back with a clearer head is *pacing*, not avoiding.

Here's the distinction in action:

- Strategic delay: You skip cleaning your apartment today in anticipation of taking an exam you have tomorrow. Smart move.

- Procrastination: You spend hours watching videos on minimalist apartments rather than cleaning your own, all while muttering, "I'll get to it. eventually."

One is helpful. The other only contributes to stress.

It is important that you recognize procrastination for what it really is: not a lack of intentionality or capability, but rather *a lack of follow-through*.

That's what makes procrastination uniquely frustrating. You're not being blocked by anything—*you're actively dodging*. And somehow, that dodging feels justified… until it doesn't.

While all this is happening, more often than not, overthinking is part of the equation. Let me explain:

The Trap of Overthinking (The Paralysis of Mental Looping)

Overthinking is when thinking no longer serves a purpose *and becomes a trap*. It's the incessant, unnecessary mental spinning that stalls action or decision-making.

Much like procrastination is vastly different from prioritization, overthinking is also vastly different from reflection. Healthy reflection is intentional—*it gets you somewhere*. You think, you learn, you choose, you move forward. Overthinking, on the other hand, just loops. It goes round and round the same thoughts, trying to predict every contingency, insuring against every danger, or getting every detail right. By the time you're "ready," the moment has already passed, and the opportunity has been lost.

Overthinking loves to masquerade as productivity: "I'm just being thorough." "I'm planning ahead." "I'm not procrastinating, *I'm preparing*." But if you've been stuck in the same thought cycle for 30 minutes and haven't made a single decision, it becomes very hard to refer to that "progress."

What it is, is paralysis.

Here are a few other familiar disguises that overthinking comes in:

- Indecision: Worrying over every possible alternative to the point where even the simplest actions feel like moves of tectonic proportions.

- Perfectionism: Editing the same sentence, spreadsheet, or message for hours because it's "not quite right yet."

- Catastrophizing: Speculating about what might go wrong and treating it as fact.

The reward? Emotional exhaustion, mental clutter, and an ever-growing reluctance to act, because *everything feels heavier than it is*.

Overthinking is your mind working against you. Your thoughts shift from being tools to being pitfalls. When the goal becomes *certainty*, *absolute control*, or *zero risk*, the mind simply keeps spinning over and over, and ultimately nothing is achieved.

You may probably wonder – why is it that procrastination goes hand in hand with overthinking despite them being fundamentally different?

I'll explain:

Two Sides of the Same Coin: How They Interact Without Being the Same

Overthinking and procrastination often show up together. But as is clear from our definition of both, they're quite different from each other. It makes sense to think of them as being more like dysfunctional roommates as opposed to twins/similar siblings: always feeding off of, and drawing energy from the worst of each other, all while being very different beasts.

Procrastination is about inaction—the task is left incomplete/sits untouched. Overthinking, on the other hand, is about mental overload—the mind won't stop spinning around and rehashing the task. *One is the body stalled, the other is the mind racing.*

If we were to use a car analogy; procrastination is like leaving the car in park when it should be moving. Overthinking, meanwhile, is flooring the gas while the parking gear is engaged. The engine's revving and burning fuel, but you're going nowhere. When you put them together, you end up with a noisy, overheating mess... and no progress. Together, procrastination and overthinking *form the procrastination-overthinking loop*, which we'll refer to simply as "The Loop" moving forward.

It starts with a task. You put it off; maybe out of fear, uncertainty, or just doubt. So, you overthink: What if I do it incorrectly? What is the optimal way to go about it? What will people think? That mental whirlpool keeps growing in intensity, so you keep going... and delay the task even more. The longer you wait, the more pressure mounts, leading to more anxious thinking.

Let me give an illustration:

You need to make a call about a billing error. But then comes the overthinking:

"What if they're rude?"
"What if I sound like an idiot?"
"Maybe I'll wait until I've rehearsed the entire conversation several times."

So, you delay.

Next day? The bill's still there. But now it's joined by guilt. Enter phase two:

"They're going to think I'm irresponsible, waiting this long to reach out."
"Now I *really* need a perfect excuse."

Day three: zero action, plenty of spiraling. And so on, and so forth.

The irony here, is that both feel positive in the moment. Overthinking feels like you're genuinely engaging with the task at hand. But really, what it is, is a clever detour of responsibility. Procrastination, on the other hand, feels like you're taking a break—but it is usually driven by all that inner chaos behind the scenes.

It needs saying that while the two often come as a package deal, they don't necessarily appear together all the time. You can overthink without avoiding (classic avoidance), and you can avoid without overthinking (think: endless mental rehearsals with constant, if disjointed, action).

It is crucial that you understand their dynamic. They are two different gears in the same jammed machine, and repairing one oftentimes necessitates *observing how it's entangled with the other*.

Up next, we build on our understanding of procrastination and overthinking and how they feed off of each other by dissecting their inner mechanics.

We'll dive into the internal experience of procrastination and overthinking—how it feels, the stories and narratives we tell ourselves, and why relying only on willpower is bound to not work. We'll examine the intangible emotional drivers that hold us back, unpack the mental narratives that keep us stuck in the loop, and learn how to shift from self-judgment to self-awareness.

Let's get to it.

Understanding What/How They Feel Like Internally

Procrastination and overthinking, in addition to being behaviors, are full-body experiences too. It's important that you understand what/how they feel like so you're able to catch them easier and faster before they can keep feeding off of each other and get exacerbated.

Procrastination often begins with a soft hum of dread. You know you've got something you "should" be doing, but the thought of it puts a knot in your stomach. You *may feel anxious* about getting started, then *guilty* that you're not getting started, then *shame* that you still aren't getting started. You keep reaching for distractions—your phone, snacks, random chores—anything to dodge the task while pretending you'll get to it "soon."

Overthinking feels markedly different—but no less stifling. It is the brain going into overdrive, trying to solve or know beforehand, every metric and potential outcome before taking the first step. You may feel *restless*, and even feel like you're getting important stuff done, but your mind is in constant orbit when it should be landing. Thoughts accumulate. Stress builds, and while you are mentally engaged, you feel emotionally drained.

Understanding how these patterns feel from the inside is crucial, because they typically masquerade behind facades of indiscipline or lack of willpower. But what they actually are, *are tangled emotional responses*—guilt and shame, perfectionism and fear, self-doubt— usually playing out in slow motion. Understanding what that feels like is step one towards disrupting the cycle before it takes hold.

Next up, we explore the narratives we tell ourselves as we allow procrastination and overthinking to begin, grow and steadily feed off of each other to the point where they take over our psyches.

The Mental Narratives We Tell Ourselves

Procrastination and overthinking usually don't begin with action—or inaction—*they start with a narrative*. And these narratives sound perfectly rational in the moment. That's what makes them effective at keeping us stalled and stuck.

Take the classic: "I'll do it later." You're not refusing to act; you're merely putting off the task with good intentions (of working on it later). "Later" always has more space, more possibility, more motivation. Of course, when later arrives, it just so happens to look a great deal like now does—but we nonetheless tell ourselves the very same thing again.

And then there's "I need more time to plan." Responsible-sounding, right? Except there's nothing responsible about using planning as an excuse for making actual progress. The work never gets done—it just gets dressed up in spreadsheets, color-coded to-do lists, an open browser with numerous tabs, etc. Planning turns into a procrastination ritual, not preparation.

Or "I won't start until it's perfect." This is the overthinker's favorite standby. Perfection becomes a prerequisite for action instead of the result of iteration. Fear of a bad first step causes the project to remain in your head forever—safe from judgment, but also safe from completion.

These narratives we tell ourselves are, more than anything, coping mechanisms—cleverly evasive ways in which we protect ourselves from *suffering, fear of failure*, and *uncertainty* (more on these in the next chapter.) And they're very common too; everybody grapples with these voices and narratives, from students to CEOs. As such, you're most certainly not alone in this.

To wrap this one up, the problem is not that these thoughts exist—it's that we automatically believe them without scrutiny. We believe them to be true instead of what they are: transient brain fog trying to keep us "safe" from danger of feeling. And the issue with this, is that safety and growth rarely – if ever – coexist.

And no, sheer willpower will not help you!

Up next, we explore why sheer willpower –something that gurus all over the internet recommend – is most certainly NOT the solution to eliminating procrastination and overthinking.

Why Willpower Isn't the Solution

The willpower myth runs deep, as far as eliminating procrastination goes. It implies that if we only grit our teeth harder—toughed it out, pushed past pain, balled our fists tighter—we'd get the job done. The problem though, is that willpower is quite akin to, say, a phone battery. It drains quickly, especially when spread thin with running "apps" in the background: *indecision*, *fear of failure*, *brain exhaustion*, etc. Trying to run your life solely by willpower is like caffeine-fueling yourself on espresso shots in an effort to stay wide awake forever. You'll inevitably burn out. Hard.

Besides, brute-force action *without knowing why you're avoiding something* just manufactures more inner resistance. Willpower may get you to start, but it won't help you stick around when discomfort rears its head—and discomfort always rears its head.

The way to beat procrastination and overthinking is not via brute-force action. You won't eliminate the procrastination-overthinking loop by willing yourself to be "stronger." If willpower was the answer, then you wouldn't be reading this. This explains why shame-based, grit-based, or empty motivational slogans fall flat. They only hit the symptom and not the underlying framework. The way to beat it, is to focus on being smarter at how you respond to inner resistance… to focus on finding out the covert reasons – those ones that you've not yet defined, much less resolved – that cause you to delay.

This book will show you how to go about this. But before we can get to that, you have to redefine the procrastination-overthinking issue in your psyche first, because only then will you put yourself in the driver's seat to deal with it effectively. We explore this next.

Redefining the Problem (From Self-Judgment to Self-Awareness)

Procrastination and overthinking often come with a heavy side of self-loathing. "Why can't I just do this?" "What is wrong with me?" These questions may sound like honest attempts at being accountable, but truly, they are merely emotional sinkholes disguised as discipline.

Let's be clear: labeling yourself as broken, undisciplined, or whatever else doesn't fix the issue—in fact, *it is part of the problem*. Self-torment can feel productive ("At least I'm being tough on myself!"), but it usually just leaves you drained, all while remaining as stuck as before.

Which brings is to this: what if, instead of judging these behaviors, *you treated them as cues*? Procrastination might be pointing to fear, exhaustion, or misalignment. Overthinking might be trying to safeguard you against uncertainty or rejection. They're not effective strategies for sure, *but they're not random malfunctions either*. They're attempts, misguided as they are, to cope.

This, however, is not to mean that you coddle yourself or make excuses. It means shifting from *blame* to *curiosity*. Instead of asking, "Why am I like this?" you ask, "What's actually happening here?" That small pivot opens the door to real insight. When you remove judgment, you create space to notice the patterns without getting buried by them. And that puts you in an actual position to deal with these patterns and behaviors in apt fashion.

With everything we've covered thus far, you now have a clear picture of what procrastination and overthinking actually are—not just how they feel, but how they function. You understand the narratives we tell ourselves, the loops we get stuck in, why brute force won't save us, and how focusing on finding out – and dealing with – the underlying reasons/drivers of our delaying behaviors and patterns.

Which brings us to the following: what *exactly* are these underlying reasons/drivers of our delaying behaviors and patterns? What's going on beneath the surface? That's exactly where we're headed next. Chapter 2 gets into this.

CHAPTER 2

THE HIDDEN CAUSES OF DELAY

As far as procrastination goes, the delay of tasks is just the visible smoke… the real fire that causes the delay is somewhere else, entirely. This chapter uncovers what's behind the stall; not the surface-level excuses, and most certainly not the quick-fix labels that too many gurus focus on, but the actual root mechanisms—the psychological reasons and drivers that we usually don't notice, because we don't know to look for them in the first place.

Let's get to it.

Reason #1: Fear in Disguise

Specifically, there are three kinds of fear that keep you stalled and stuck in the loop: *fear of failure, fear of judgment* and *fear of success*:

Fear of failure is the old boogeyman. You don't do the task because it's difficult, but because falling at it *could make an underlying fear a* *reality*: Perhaps I'm not good enough. Perhaps I'm just not cut out for this. Etc. So, rather than confront that probability, your brain would rather do something else; perhaps rearrange your kitchen spice rack, begin a new side project, etc.

Fear of judgment works quite similarly. You're not only concerned about failing, you're also (perhaps even more) concerned *about being caught failing*. That article draft remains unwritten because what if someone reads it and says, "That's it?' So, your brain chooses to delay than risk exposure.

Then there's the **fear of success**—yes, really. Because success isn't just a happy ending: it may mean greater pressure, more eyes, more expectations, etc. You land one good gig, and suddenly you're expected to keep delivering at that level. It's safer not to take that risk; to stall and stay small, than risk getting overwhelmed by "what comes next."

What makes these fears so very hard to recognize and pin down is they tend to slip in as "reasonable" thoughts:

"I need to research and learn and more."
"I will start when I feel more confident."
"I want to do it right the first time."

They seem responsible. But they're often anything but.

Reason #2: Identity Conflict
(When the Task Clashes with Who We Think We Are)

Procrastination usually isn't about the task itself, but rather about what doing that task reveals about us. Sometimes, our procrastination indicates a deeper conflict between *what we need to do and who we think we are*.

Think about those internal voices you may have from time to time, many of which feed off of procrastination in the first place:

"I'm not a disciplined person."
"I'm not creative enough for this."
"I'm not a leader."

A lot of the time, these statements go beyond being excuses. They become descriptions of how we perceive (or how we've learned over a period of time to view) ourselves. When a task contradicts that image, going ahead with it almost feels like betrayal. *You can't be someone you're not without inwardly rebelling against it.*

This identity conflict creates a subtle albeit really powerful barrier that keeps you stuck and unable to act progressively. Think of trying to run a marathon while wearing a pair of shoes two sizes too small. Your feet will hurt, and eventually, you'll stop. Similarly, when your actions don't match your internal story, your motivation cramps up and you're unable to proceed.

What is more, this resistance typically acts as self-protection. Maintaining a consistent identity, *even a flawed one*, feels safer and preferable to going into the uncharted territory of modifying your sense of yourself.

The good news here though, is that *identity is not fixed*. It's a story you can edit and rewrite. That too many of us don't understand this, is a major reason why we're often unable to shake off procrastination, along with other undesirable habits and perceptions of ourselves that we've picked up over the years. But to do so, you have to recognize how far your present story might be limiting you. Once you understand that your procrastination may be based on identity conflict, it'll instantly open the door to shifting the way you think about yourself— and what you believe you can do.

Reason #3: Task Aversion and Emotional Avoidance

A lot of the time when we procrastinate, we're not avoiding the task itself, but rather the unpleasant emotions it stirs up. The task is a trigger for feelings we'd rather not face (think boredom, frustration, confusion, uncertainty, etc.)

Here's an example: Think of the last time you procrastinated on something important. Say, your budget. If you look deeper into it, you'll see that it's not the math or the spreadsheets that freeze you, but rather the shame or anxiety or fear about your finances. In this regard, the task becomes a gateway to those uncomfortable emotions, and our brain's natural reflex is to steer clear.

This emotional avoidance explains why some tasks feel so heavy, even when you know at heart that they're technically simple (or are at least supposed to be.) It becomes a shield of protection from the unease and discomfort that these tasks put us in. So, we tell ourselves, "I'll deal with it later." But really, what we're saying to ourselves is, "I'm not ready to meet these feelings."

The next time you procrastinate, and ask yourself—not "Why am I procrastinating on this task?"—but "What emotions am I avoiding here?" You may discover a whole lot about yourself, and the specific factors that are causing you to procrastinate.

Reason #4: Decision Fatigue and Choice Overload

In today's world, it's not too uncommon for every day to feel like a never-ending onslaught of choices: what to eat for breakfast, what email to open first, what program to use, how to organize and schedule a project, etc. The sheer scale of the quantity of options is bound to exhaust even the most resilient minds. This mental exhaustion is what is known as *decision fatigue*, and it's a potent, surreptitious cause of procrastination. Let's unpack this:

When our minds become overburdened, we lose direction and focus, and this causes us to stall instead of moving forward. Think of trying to get started on a project but stalling because you can't choose which software program to run, what step to attempt first, or even what the final product ought to look like. The project itself isn't overwhelming—*the numerous micro-decisions that surround it are.* Each decision, on its own, may be small, but collectively they drain our willpower and clog our mental bandwidth.

Reason #5: Low Clarity, Low Action

Ambiguity is a procrastinator's best friend. When goals, steps, or priorities aren't clear, *our brain struggles to pick a direction*, and that's when delay creeps in.

Consider this: Have you ever stared at a task, feeling, "I should do something, but I don't know what exactly"? That vague, nebulous sense of "do something" is a mental block disguised as busywork. In the absence of clarity, *motivation evaporates* and inaction inevitably sets in.

Compare that to simple, well-defined tasks. When you know precisely what to do next—send one email, complete one form, or write two paragraphs—you are able to move faster. Simple steps cut the overwhelming into bite-sized chunks, in so doing providing your brain with a clear-cut path to take.

Oftentimes, low clarity comes from broad, abstract goals like "Get fit," or complex projects with no clear first move ("Improve my business", etc.) Without direction, your brain defaults to delay as a way to avoid confusion and overwhelm.

Reason #6: Lack of Internal Relevance (When the Task Feels Empty)

We tend to assume that important or critical tasks automatically get done. However, far too often, those same tasks remain untouched for long periods of time. Why? *Because they don't resonate on a personal, emotional level with us.*

We resist even what know to be objectively necessary—a deadline, a utility bill, a report that must be written, etc.—*if it feels hollow or meaningless inside*. Our brain doesn't just respond to external importance; it craves internal relevance too. Without that, motivation tends to dry up and delay sets in.

This disconnect often happens with tasks imposed to us by others: bosses, teachers, family, societal expectations, et al. These external pressures create a mental tug-of-war. The task exists "out there," but our inner self rejects it, *seeing it as someone else's priority, not ours*. This rejection is a silent refusal… *a subconscious rebellion expressed through delay*.

For example, you may find yourself procrastinating on a work project because you don't truly believe in its value or purpose. Or you put off studying material that feels disconnected from/irrelevant to your goals or interests, even when you know it's critical for passing a course. *The task doesn't resonate emotionally, so it's bumped down the pecking order of your priority list*.

Reason #7: Learned Helplessness and Past Failure Conditioning

When you fail or are harshly criticized regularly, such experiences tend to leave a mark deeper than simple frustration. Over time, they can eventually mold a "why bother?" attitude, where trying seems meaningless due to the apparent inevitability that whatever you do will be negative/disapproved of. This is known as *learned helplessness*: a conditioned belief that you will never manage to succeed, whatever you do.

In this state, procrastination becomes a subtle mechanism of self-defense. By delaying or not acting, you protect yourself from the pain and hurt that may result from failure. The mind tries to avoid disappointment by proactively retreating from effort, almost as if saying, "If I don't do this, I can't fail. Success may be out of the option, but the again so is failure." This learned pattern often leads to self-sabotage, and you may find yourself increasingly hesitating, stalling, or giving up early because of your past conditioning. Importantly, this is a deep, automatic response, often unconscious and, at its core, *an evolved survival mechanism.*

This response can lead to a discouraging cycle: previous failures fuel learned helplessness, which accelerates delay, which heightens the likelihood of additional disappointment, perpetuating the cycle.

Reason #8: Energy Deficit and Poor Recovery Cycles

Sometimes, delay isn't tethered to psychological elements or mind-blocks. Sometimes, it's physical – rooted in the state of your body and brain. When your energy stores get low, no amount of motivation or willpower can or will push through beyond the natural drop in productivity. Fatigue will pull down focus, clarity, and stamina.

Basic biological and neurologic factors are responsible here. Bad sleep diminishes your brain's capacity to regulate attention and decision-making. Bad nutrition deprives your body of fuel to support concentrated effort. Dopamine burnout, resulting from chronic stress or overstimulation, numbs your motivation and reward system. *All these add up to an energy deficit that sabotages action.*

This, in fact, is often the most overlooked cause of delay, and ignoring physical and neurological needs leads to a cycle of exhaustion and avoidance, where tasks feel overwhelming because your system lacks the resources to engage.

This is why it is important that you spread your focus to energy cycles, and understanding the physical rhythms of your body, in addition to time management, in your bid to combat and eliminate procrastination. Because once you understand the ebbs and flows of your energy, you will have a much clearer perspective on why some days are so productive while others are woefully unproductive.

With all this covered, it begs the question: what happens when all these hidden causes of delay—fear, identity conflict, emotional avoidance, decision fatigue, low clarity, internal relevance, learned helplessness, and energy deficits—feed off our stress? What happens is that instead of just slowing us down, they greatly amplify the pressure and anxiety, creating a really vicious cycle that can make it incredibly difficult to get out of our stalled state.

The next chapter goes deep into this.

CHAPTER 3

THE STRESS–PROCRASTINATION CYCLE

Procrastination often feels like a way to avoid stress—but in essence, it just makes stress worse. You avoid a task, feel some temporary relief for it, deadlines approach nonetheless, since the task remains undone; guilt builds, discomfort grows, clarity is steadily lost, which leads to more task avoidance, etc. This creates a self-reinforcing pattern: *stress leads to delay, and delay leads to more stress*.

This chapter breaks down how that cycle works, how it feeds into itself, and why it's so ubiquitous.

Let's get to it.

How Stress Triggers Delay

When stress levels rise, the brain shifts into survival mode. The prefrontal cortex—responsible for *planning*, *reasoning*, and *decision-making*—takes a back seat. Instead, the brain activates the amygdala, which drives the *fight*, *flight*, or *freeze response*. In this state, you're not primed to think ahead or weigh long-term benefits. *All your mental resources are primarily wired to seek safety and immediate relief.*

This shift impacts behavior directly, and brings us to the initial procrastination phase. Presented with a task that appears overwhelming, complex, or unclear, your brain perceives it as a threat. Instead of moving toward it, you might flee (avoid it), freeze (get paralyzed by uncertainty), or fight (redirect your frustration elsewhere). None of these steps complete the task—*but all of them temporarily ease your sense of pressure.*

Procrastination, in this regard, is a direct response to stress. When you choose to glance at your phone, watch a video, or clean up your desk instead of answering that pressing email, you are choosing an immediate elimination of discomfort. Your brain offers you a reward of a moment of relief for it, reinforcing the delay.

That is why stressful tasks—especially those with high-stakes, unclear instructions, or affective load—are the kind that we procrastinate on the most. Procrastination itself becomes a coping mechanism; *a concerted attempt to control the stress rather than the work.*

But understanding that stress often leads to procrastination (and how it does so) is only the beginning—what keeps us stuck is how deceptively comforting avoidance can feel in the moment. We explore this next.

The False Relief: Why Avoidance Feels Good... Briefly

Procrastination often feels like a solution—*because, for a moment, it is*. When you're stressed by a task, avoiding it creates a sharp drop in tension. That drop feels like relief. The brain gets aware of this. It takes note: Avoiding this made me feel better.

This creates a feedback loop. Stress builds up → you evade the task → stress dissipates → brain reinforces the behavior. Same pattern for habits like stress-eating or scrolling aimlessly. Discomfort passes briefly, *so your brain records avoidance as a success*. Although the task is still out there, instant discomfort is erased—*and that's what the brain prefers*.

This cycle is reinforced chemically, too. When you avoid something stressful, your brain reduces the amount of stress chemicals, like cortisol, that it releases. While doing this, it may also release more dopamine—the pleasure and reward chemical—especially if you transition to something pleasurable or anesthetizing (like surfing social media or watching video). You've essentially shifted from tension to comfort. *The contrast makes the reward that much stronger*.

As time passes, your brain starts to directly link certain avoidance behaviors with comforting emotions. Scrolling through your phone, snacking, pacing, tidying, even daydreaming—*these become unconscious mechanisms of tension-release*. The more you employ them, the more automatic they get, which only leads to the amplification of stress, as time passes, since the task(s) still remain untouched. More on this, next.

How Procrastination Amplifies Stress

Procrastination gives temporary relief, but that comes at the cost of compounded stress. Once the initial relief is over, the task remains—only now, it's *closer*, *heavier*, and *more urgent*. That which was initially just discomfort becomes outright pressure... time has shrunk, expectations haven't changed one bit, and your margin for error has grown considerably smaller and smaller with the passage of time.

Psychologically, the weight of tasks left undone starts to grow too. It lingers in the background, creating a steady, increasingly taut tension even when you're not actively thinking about it. This is known as "*task residue.*" It is the mental clutter of uncompleted work, and it quietly (and quickly) drains attention and energy.

Added to all this, is guilt. With each delay, not only are you avoiding the task—you are adding self-judgment to the heap. You start questioning your self-discipline, lagging behind schedule, dreading being exposed as irresponsible or unprepared, etc. That guilt, it goes without saying, is useless... crippling even. And the more of it you feel, the more it is tempting to procrastinate once again—feeding the same cycle.

Then there's anticipatory stress. This is the stress of anticipation of what's coming but hasn't yet arrived... the mental noise of what hasn't yet happened—missed deadlines, disappointed people, unfinished projects, etc.—but might happen at any time. Anticipatory stress activates the very same fight-or-flight circuits as imminent threats, even though nothing has happened yet, meaning that *your body and brain respond as if you're already under threat.*

The task itself hasn't changed. *What's changed is your relationship with it.* It now carries emotional baggage, urgency, and negative expectation. What began as an attempt to minimize stress has instead created a psychological storm that intensifies the closer you get to the moment of reckoning. In this way, procrastination doesn't remove the stress—it only delays it, then intensifies it by attaching urgency, guilt and fear to it. And best believe the cycle will continue, up until it is directly addressed. With this covered, the next step is to examine the real-life stressors that kick this whole cycle into gear.

Everyday Triggers That Set the Cycle in Motion

The stress–procrastination cycle often begins before we're even aware of it. Certain conditions quietly set the stage, making it more likely we'll enter the cycle without realizing it.

Overcommitment is one of the primary stimuli. Taking on too much stretches energy and attention thin. When everything appears urgent, little to nothing gets done. Work accumulates, tension builds, and the avoidance cycle kicks in.

Lack of control—over your environment, workload, or schedule—also perpetuates stress. When you don't feel in charge of your choices or time, *tasks feel imposed rather than voluntary*. This feeling of loss of control increases pressure and decreases motivation.

Constant interruptions fragment attention. Every time you're pulled away—by messages, calls, people, et al—your brain spends effort refocusing. That drain adds up, making even simple tasks feel harder. With diminished focus comes mounting frustration and the urge to disengage.

Unrealistic expectations, either self-imposed or external, fuel perfectionism. The belief that a task must be completed flawlessly creates a lot of internal pressure. Instead of starting, the mind stalls—waiting for ideal conditions or fearing failure. Avoidance then masquerades as planning or "waiting until you're ready."

The **Inability to say no** traps you in obligations you never fully committed to. Saying yes out of guilt or fear fosters resentment, especially if your plate was already full to begin with. That emotional weight totals up to stress and drains the motivation to act.

It's important that you understand that these triggers aren't the same for everybody. Your triggers will be different to those of someone else, etc. As such, you need to assess your life closely. Which ones do you encounter most often? What patterns do you recognize? Once you're aware of what pulls you in, the cycle becomes a lot easier to observe—and, ultimately, to break.

Up next, we explore the cognitive and physiological impacts that the stress-procrastination cycle has on us.

CHAPTER 4

THE COGNITIVE AND PHYSIOLOGICAL IMPACTS OF THE STRESS-PROCRASTINATION CYCLE

C hronic stress does more than affect your emotional base—*it also directly affects the way you think* as well as how your physical body functions. This chapter delves into all this, in comprehensive detail. It explores how the stress-procrastination cycle affects your overall behavior, *even away from the task*, without you even knowing it.

Let's get the ball rolling.

The Cognitive Impact (How Stress Shrinks Perspective)

Under stress, the brain drastically narrows its focus. As we highlighted in the previous chapter, all of the brain's attention and resources *are diverted to survival and threat management*, and not comprehension or creative problem-solving. So, thinking becomes overly static, repetitive, and negative/pessimistic. Options seem fewer, solutions less available, and confidence/self-assurance dips.

Negative thinking increases because stress-biased attention primarily focuses on what could go wrong. You tend to only spot the dangers, the flaws, the "what ifs", et al, and this creates mental paralysis instead of readiness. Flexibility drops and the ability to change perspective or try alternative approaches drops to zero. *You become mentally stuck in a steady worry-based frame of reference.*

Creativity also suffers. Your mind does not have space to explore new connections or new possibilities if it is clogged with stress signals. The capacity to redefine problems and break them up into actionable steps, as such, is blocked. That gives rise to black-and-white thinking: either there's *flawless execution or utter failure*, and that double pressure further makes procrastination more likely.

Stress also fuels overthinking. Your mind keeps on rehearsing the task, running endless loops of worst-case scenarios, and doubting your ability to handle it. The more you overthink, the harder it becomes to accomplish the task—even if it hasn't changed at all.

This generates what's referred to as *task inflation*… when tension distorts perception and makes tasks seem larger, more complex, or more threatening than they actually are. Responding to an email feels like a confrontation, a short form feels like a legal exam, etc. Inflated perception sustains avoidance, which generates pressure, and so the cycle goes on.

So, stress does not simply cause discomfort—it massively warps perception too. It *overstates difficulty*, *discourages resourcefulness*, and *tightens the mental bandwidth* available to respond with acuity. It also has a significant impact on our physical bodies as well. We explore this next.

The Physiological Side (What Happens in the Body)

Stress doesn't just stay in the brain—it unfolds throughout the entire body too. As soon as your brain senses danger, whether it's an impending deadline or too much to do in too little time, it launches a physiological chain reaction. Cortisol, the body's major stress hormone, surges. Heart rate accelerates, muscles tense, and energy stores are diverted for a possible "fight or flight" response.

This alertness is not built for long durations. When stress becomes chronic (lasts for too long), cortisol levels remain elevated for longer than the human body is adapted to, disrupting various systems of the body. Muscles become tensed, often leading to headaches, jaw pain, and tense shoulders. Sleep is shallow or even interrupted. You may wake up tired, feel drowsy during the day, and experience energy crashes that badly drain motivation.

Stress fatigue is not only physical, it's neurological too. The brain demands and consumes more glucose while under pressure, but the stress diminishes its capacity to effectively utilize that energy. The end result is usually unending mental fatigue. Things that would typically have a moderate energy demand begin to seem heavy and impossible to handle.

Under this state, motivation tends to suffer naturally. Concentration is harder, planning is tougher, and sustaining attention is a lot more challenging, as the body signals you to conserve energy or escape the perceived threat. Procrastination becomes a physiological need and psychological habit at the same time. Instead of working through the tension, the body and brain gravitate towards temporary relief—anything that provides relaxation or distraction from the discomfort and pressure.

This is where the feedback loop becomes deeper. The longer the body is stressed, the more it will signal withdrawal. *And the more you withdraw, the less you will act—adding to the stress.*

Now that we've seen what's going on under the hood, let's shift to examining why trying harder and forcing the issue often backfires and only leads to amplified stress levels.

Why Trying Harder Often Backfires

The previous chapter explained why sheer grit and willpower rarely work to break the *procrastination-overthinking* loop. When it comes to the *stress-procrastination* cycle, not only does pushing harder rarely work, it also often backfires spectacularly.

Let's break this down:

Stress erodes self-regulation directly. The prefrontal cortex's executive processes, such as impulse regulation, emotion regulation, and sustained attention don't operate very well under stress. So, the harder you push when already under mental strain, the higher your risk of snapping, freezing, or hitting the avoidance spin cycle *even harder than before*.

Then shame kicks in. You think, "I must be able to do this." You hold yourself up against the mental ideal of who you believe you're supposed to be—keen, alert, in control—and feel like you're falling short. That self-judgment supercharges emotions on top of an already overwrought system. You're no longer just overwhelmed by tasks; you're also overwhelmed by *what those tasks seem to say* about your worthiness or ability.

This is when the cycle gets well and truly reinforced. You begin to associate effort with frustration and failure. Striving harder becomes emotionally draining. Each time you fail, it reinforces the idea that you are lazy or broken, when, in reality, you are just running on a system pushed beyond what's sustainable.

As such, when you are off kilter—constantly stressed, sleep-starved, emotionally drained—more force isn't going to do the trick. It usually just rams the wedge deeper.

With everything that we've covered thus far, it is imperative that you understand that the first crack in any cycle *is awareness*. You can't interrupt and halt what you can't see. The stress-procrastination cycle runs on autopilot—thoughts racing, pressure building, avoidance offering instant (but temporary) relief. But when you're able to see the pattern when you're in it, everything changes.

Most of all, awareness creates space. And in that space, other choices are possible. Certainly not easy—but certainly a lot more possible.

And this is where our next section, Section 2, begins. Section 2 will help you learn, in a clear, simple and straightforward manner, how to interrupt the procrastination-overthinking and stress-procrastination loops *consistently* by leveraging smarter, better habits that turn the cycle completely on its head.

SECTION 2

ESCAPING THE LOOP – RESET AND REWIRE

Section 1 provided great insight into procrastination, why it happens and how it affects us. This section helps you turn all the insight you picked up into action to effectively beat procrastination. Here, you'll learn how to interrupt the cycle of overthinking and delay by mastering your thoughts, emotions, and energy levels. We'll cover how to reset anxious or negative thought patterns, how to manage emotional spikes that derail your day, and how to stay consistent even when motivation is missing. You'll also discover the keys to time *and* energy management—because managing minutes without managing your mental fuel *is a losing game*.

Let's get to it.

CHAPTER 5

REWIRING YOUR THOUGHTS TO HELP BEAT PROCRASTINATION

The first step to beating procrastination is rewiring how you *think*, and replacing negative loops *with action-oriented ones*. This chapter has been put together with the goal of helping you *pause long enough to recognize what's actually happening in your mind*. Before you can change your thoughts, you have to see them clearly, and this chapter helps you do just that via *6 actionable steps*.

Let's get started.

I: Challenge the Delay Narrative (Thought ≠ Truth)

To challenge and neutralize delay-driving thoughts, follow this exact step-by-step procedure. And don't wait for conviction, or until you "feel primed enough" to do it either—just follow the steps. The last thing you want to do is *procrastinate the process for beating procrastination*.

Step 1: Catch the Thought in the Moment

Start noticing the exact words and phrasing that run through your mind before procrastinating. Write it down—verbatim. Precision is crucial here.

Here are some examples:

- *"I don't have time to do it now."*
- *"I need to wait until I'm more focused."*
- *"I already messed up the day, might as well start tomorrow."*

Step 2: Label It— "This Is a Script"

Don't engage with it. Just say, "This is a mental script." Not a truth and most certainly not a command/stipulation. All it is, is a recycled line that your brain throws out.

Do this out loud if necessary; the physical act of labeling can be quite effective for breaking auto-obedience.

Step 3: Run the 3-Question Filter

Challenge the script with these specific questions:

1. *"Is this 100% true?"*
2. *"Where does this thought usually lead?"*
3. *"What will happen if I ignore it and just start anyway?"*

It's important that you do not overthink this one—try and respond as quickly and honestly as you can.

Step 4: Rewrite the Script on Paper (Short, Actionable)

Take the original line and write a counter-script that *you can act on now*, not *one that necessarily feels motivational*. Keep it as short and specific as possible.

Here are a few examples:

- Instead of "*I don't have time*,"
  → "*I have 7 minutes. I'll use them to the best of my ability*."

- Instead of "*I need to feel ready*,"
  → "*Action creates readiness. I start small*."

- Instead of "*It has to be perfect*,"
  → "*Version 1, not perfection. Just draft*."

Step 5: Do One Tiny Physical Action Immediately

Open the tab. Write one sentence. Move the file. Just one physical motion right after rewriting the script. This anchors the new pattern.

Example Walkthrough to Illustrate the Steps Above:

It's 5:42 PM. You think, "The day's already off-track, I'll regroup tomorrow."

- You label it: *Script*.

- You challenge: *Not true. This leads to more delay. Acting now is still progress*.

- You rewrite: "*One action now means I didn't quit the day*."

- You open your notes app and write a single bullet point for the task/perform one specific bit, however small, of the task at hand.

And just like that, you challenge the narrative instantly and create momentum.

II: Focus on the Process, *Not the Outcome*

A lot of the time when we procrastinate, it's usually because the finish line seems enormous. The brain only perceives the gap from now and done, and subsequently clams up. The trick is to cease aiming at "*done*" and start aiming at "*show up*." Lower your sights, as opposed to lowering your standards:

Step 1: Notice the Outcome Language

Catch yourself when your inner voice is loaded with pressure to complete, win, or impress. It typically sounds like this:

- *"I have to get this done today."*
- *"This needs to be perfect."*
- *"If I don't get it perfect, it is not worth doing."*

Statements like these fuel fear, *not productivity*. The brain interprets them as risk, as we explored in the previous section, and this causes avoidance.

Step 2: Recondition It to Time-Based Process Language

Replace outcome-heavy phrasing with action-based, low-stakes cues. The structure is:

"I'm not trying to finish this. I'm just showing up for X minutes."

Here are a few examples:

- *"I'm going to work on this for 25 minutes."*
- *"I'll sketch out a rough outline, nothing final."*
- *"Just one round of focused effort—then I'll reassess."*

Keep it light, small, and time-boxed and make NO promises *beyond the effort itself.*

Step 3: Work with a Visible Timer—Not for Pressure, but for Containment

Set a visible countdown. It reminds you that this isn't endless; it's bounded and contained.

- 15 to 30 minutes is adequate for most high-resistance tasks.

- Think of it as not measuring performance, but *measuring presence* instead.

Step 4: Close with a Micro-Win Reminder

Whenever your time block runs out, record what you did—however small it is/was.

For example: "*Wrote 2 paragraphs*." Or, "*Organized project notes*."

This reinforces and verifies that productivity is not perfection, *but progress.*

Here's a brief example to illustrate the steps above:

Instead of "*I have to clean out the entire garage today.*"

Substitute with: "*I'm going to sort one shelf for 25 minutes and see how far I get.*"

You set the timer. You toss a few items. You label one bin: "Donate."

In this way, the pressure of outcome reduces all while the process builds.

III: Shrink the Mental Load with Precise Language

Overwhelm isn't always so much about the task at hand as it is about *how we frame it in our minds*. Unclear thinking like "*This is too much*" or "*Where do I even start*?" usually creates mental static. The brain is drastically slowed down trying to do and process everything at once—and ultimately accomplishes nothing.

Clarity is the fix for this. Clear, precise language breaks apart fuzzy, vague overwhelm into productive direction.

Step 1: Identify and Interpret Fuzzy Mental Language

First, catch yourself using big, vague phrasing. Phrases like:

- *"I need to get my life together"*
- *"This report is massive"*
- *"I have so much to do"*

These are mental blobs, is what they are. They don't give the brain anything specific to act on. Your job is to translate them into something physically doable.

Here are some examples of apt translation:

- *"This project is so huge"*
  → *"I'll draft the first paragraph."*

- *"I must prepare for the meeting"*
  → *"I'll make three bullet points I want to discuss."*

- *"I need to correct my resume"*
  → *"I'll correct the job title on my last position."*

Step 2: Use the One-Move Mindset

Ask yourself one question:

"What's the next visible step?"

Not the whole plan and not the outcome either; just the next small, concrete step that *can be taken visibly in the physical world.*

Here are some examples:

- *Open the file*
- *Name the document*
- *Write the first sentence*
- *Send one email*

Do that—then ask again.

Step 3: Make Language Physical, Not Abstract

Avoid abstract verbs like *"figure out"*, *"organize"*, or *"work on."*

Instead, use verbs with visible actions: *type, open, email, list, sketch, move, rename.*

Why it works: The mind processes clear verbs quicker. At the same time, having clarity eliminates resistance.

IV: Replace Shame-Based Self-Talk with Self-Instruction

When you procrastinate, your inner voice turns against you. Instead of motivating you, it criticizes:

- *"Why can't I just get this done?"*
- *"I'm such a lazy bum."*
- *"What the hell is wrong with me?"*

The issue with shame-based self-talk is that does not motivate. It paralyzes. It increases mental noise, decreases clarity, and makes the task even more ominous. What works, instead, is self-instruction— *words that encourage, not stack on the blame.*

Here's how to shift your inner speech:

Step 1: Catch the Shame Script

Observe the tone and language of your inner voice. Shame-based self-talk tends to sound accusatory and emotional. *It picks on you rather than the task in question.*

Common statements:

- *"I always make a mess of things."*
- *"This shouldn't be so difficult."*
- *"Other folks don't have problems with this."*

These are thought patterns that manifest as questions attacking identity: "What's wrong with me?" There isn't a helpful answer to an unhelpful question like that. It just sends your brain into shutdown or defense mode.

Step 2: Switch to Task-Focused, Neutral Instructions

Substitute judgmental language with calm, firm self-guidance.

New phrasing:

- *"Right now, the next logical step is to call the supplier."*
- *"I'll dial the number and ask one clear question."*
- *"I just need to start the conversation."*

Instructional speech cuts through emotional noise. It tells your brain what to do, *not how to feel*, which is what leads to delay.

Step 3: Use a Coaching Tone

Be an encouraging coach to yourself, not drill instructor, and most definitely not a critic. Your tone can be *the* make or break factor. Firm and calm beats abrupt and theatrical.

Affirmative tone:

- *"This is just a task and nothing more. I can accomplish this step by step."*
- *"Let's get back on track. No big deal."*
- *"Progress not perfection."*

Avoid trying to "feel motivated." Just give directions as if to someone you care about.

Step 4: Create a Reset Phrase

Have a default line that gets you back in when your mind becomes critical or stuck.

Here are a few examples:

- *"Let's not make this more complicated than it is. What's the next step?"*
- *"I'm not here to be perfect. I'm here to make the next step."*
- *"One step forward. That's the goal."*

Your mental script should be relaxed, grounded, and attainable.

V: Leverage Future-Self Thinking (Think Beyond the Now-Brain)

Procrastination lives and thrives in the present. The "now-brain" craves and pursues comfort and ease/relief at the moment, *even if it means giving up your higher long-term goals*. That's why scrolling, snacking, or really just about anything else may seem more attractive than starting work on a task—even one that you are genuinely eager to get started on.

To break through that fog, you *need to adopt a different point of view*. Future-self thinking allows you to get out of the discomfort you're in at the moment psychologically, and link up with a version of yourself *that has already experienced the advantage of the very thing you're procrastinating on*.

Here's how to use future-self thinking as an action-ready reboot strategy:

Step 1: Identify the Now-Brain Bias

Your brain, as we've established, *wants to avoid discomfort now, not solve problems for later*. That's why procrastination often feels logical in the moment, even when it fundamentally is anything but.

For example, you're supposed to prep slides for a presentation, but YouTube seems a lot more appealing. "I'll do it later," your brain says. It's solving *for right now*, not the deadline creeping up.

Step 2: Ask, "What Will Tomorrow Me Thank Me For?"

Shift the frame from present discomfort to short-term payoff. Make it as self-referential as possible too.

Ask:

> *"What will tomorrow-me regret if I don't do it today?"*

Keep the window small—24 hours or less. This makes it *concrete and urgent*.

For instance, let's say you don't feel like responding to emails. Nonetheless, you pause and reflect: "*If I get five done now, tomorrow me starts lighter.*" That frame gives purpose and meaning to the next small action.

Step 3: Use the Visualization Reset

If the task appears overwhelming, try this question:

> *"If it were already done, how would I feel?"*

Let yourself picture the relief, momentum, or pride—even if just for five seconds. This provides your brain *with a preview of the reward beforehand.*

For instance; you don't feel like doing your taxes. However, you picture the feeling of clicking "submit" and being done. The *pretend relief* activates a little bit of action, and you'll find it easier to open the folder and begin.

Step 4: Link Motivation to a Near Future, Not Some Distant Ideal

Don't make sweeping declarations such as "*This is part of my ten-year plan.*" That's too hypothetical. Instead, aim for instant wins and rewards with near-future returns.

For example, don't say, "This spreadsheet is going to help build my legacy." Say: "*If I get this done today, I can kick back this evening without guilt.*"

That's the real hook.

VI: Anchor to Identity (Act Like the Person You Want to Become)

Procrastination isn't just about time—it's about identity too. If you don't think you're somebody who can get things done, *then you'll act exactly like that.* The great news here is that identity isn't fixed. Rather, *it's heavily influenced by repetition.*

Understand that we're not talking about deep inner conflict (covered in Chapter 2). We're talking about *day-to-day pragmatic identity alignment.* You build new behavior by acting like the kind of person you want to be—*before it comes automatically.*

Step 1: Utilize Identity as a Proactive Tool, Not as a Fixed Designation

Most of us think that identity is discovered. In reality, however, it's something we practice. You don't wait to feel focused before getting started; you get started, and the feeling follows.

Say, you're trying to write consistently, but feel scattered. Instead of saying, "*I'm not a disciplined person,*" shift to: "*What would a focused writer do next?*" That becomes your guide and, with enough repetition, your identity.

Step 2: Ask, "What Would a Focused Person Do Right Now?"

This reset question pulls you out of your default habits *and into deliberate behavior.*

Don't debate how you're feeling. Don't wait to feel motivated. Just ask what the identity you're striving for would do—*then do that.*

For example, if you catch yourself thinking: "*I'm going to surf instead of work.*" Pause. Ask yourself: "*What would a focused, on-task person do at this moment?*" The answer is clear: they would open the document and get to working.

So, you do just that.

Step 3: Align with Action, Not Feelings

Inspiration comes and goes. *Identity-based action doesn't.* The answer isn't to be motivated—*it's to act consistently with your idealized self-image.*

You don't wait to feel like cleaning your space. You decide: "*I'm the kind of person who organizes their environment.*" You tidy up the desk, and *your action reinforces your identity.*

Step 4: Use the Mental Script: "I'm the Type of Person Who..."

Start conditioning your mind to associate action and identity.

Use it consistently, too:

> "*I'm the type of person who gets things done.*"

> "*I'm the type of person who doesn't need to be ready to act.*"

Once you do this consistently, you'll realize that far from being mere phrases, these are superb mental anchors— reminders that what you're getting ready to do next is defining who you are and who you want to become.

With all this covered, do understand that patterns *don't develop overnight.* Just as procrastination was developed through repetition, your patterns of reset must be consistently worked into place. One clear moment may not undo a decade of mental noise—but it will interrupt the pattern. The work here is not to think perfectly, *but to notice the old thought, to stop, and replace it with one that actually assists.* Do it once, then do it again and again. Your brain wants patterns and *you* get to decide which ones stick.

Now that the mental framing is addressed, the next challenge is *emotion*. Both mental framing and emotional regulation often run in parallel, so it's only logical to move from cognitive patterns to emotional mastery, so you are able to reinforce inner clarity and calm and put yourself in a superb position to beat procrastination. The next chapter explores this.

CHAPTER 6

PRACTICING EMOTIONAL CONTROL WITHOUT SUPPRESSION

A lot of the time, it's usually emotional overload—an internal system clogged with worry, frustration, self-doubt, or shame – beneath the surface that leads to procrastination (or at the very least exacerbates it.) Not that you won't/can't buckle down; you're just clogged and blocked emotionally. And while the instinct is to stuff these feelings away and "push through," we've already established that doing that doesn't work. Suppressed feelings tend to stay put, and the longer they simmer and stew, the more they hijack your attention, drain your energy, and, take control.

This chapter, in 6 highly practical steps, explores how to practice emotional control without suppression … to pay attention to what you're feeling, process it, and choose your next move so you can beat procrastination.

Let's get to it.

I: Label Before You Act: The Pause > Label > Shift Framework

Procrastination is typically driven by strong/intense emotions. But most of us aren't aware we're reacting emotionally until we're already well down the path of avoidance. That's where the **Pause** > **Label** > **Shift** model —a practical process for working with emotion *before it hijacks action* – enters the picture.

Here's how to go about it:

Step 1: Pause When the Avoidance Urge Hits

You get the urge to check your phone. Open YouTube. Scroll. And just like that, everything else seems more appealing than the task you set out to do. This is the very moment that you need to pause.

Do nothing. Don't judge. Simply pause.

Step 2: Label the Emotion Precisely

Vague, fuzzy feelings tend to have a lot of power over your proclivity to procrastinate. Labeling them—accurately and specifically too—shrinks them considerably. And this is not mere pop psych either: neuroscience shows that referring to an emotion by name greatly reduces its grip by calming the amygdala[i].

Use such language as:

- *"I'm feeling overwhelmed."*
- *"I'm afraid I'm going to blow it."*
- *"I'm embarrassed I didn't start earlier."*

For example, say, you've been avoiding a task all day. You pause, take note of the emotion and label it: "*I'm not lazy. I'm just scared of not doing well.*" That definition not only makes the feeling real—it also makes it more manageable.

Step 3: Shift from a Position of Grounded Awareness

Once the emotion's been seen and named, you're no longer reacting blindly. *You're grounded.* From this position, you can (and should) make conscious moves forward—not necessarily because the emotion went away (it will most likely still be with you), *but because you're no longer fused to it.*

Use the reset script to help you with this:

> "*I'm not unmotivated. I'm just feeling [X] right now.*"
> Then: "*Nonetheless, I can still do the next step.*"

II: Let Emotions Be Data, Not Directives

Emotions tend to be loud a lot of the time, *but they don't always yell truth*. One of the core skills in beating procrastination is the skill of listening to your emotions *but not necessarily obeying them*.

Once you learn to view your emotions as data, they instantly become useful cues. If you view them as directives, on the other hand, they quickly become barriers to progress.

Here's how to go about this one:

Step 1: Differentiate Emotion from Instruction

Just because you're in a pinch, uninspired, or exposed doesn't mean you should stop. *Emotions are internal feedback—not external mandates.*

Think of them dashboard lights: they flash a warning, but they don't outright tell you what to do next. Your job is to interpret the signal, not respond blindly to it.

For example, let's say you are nervous at the prospect of presenting. As intense as the feeling may be, it does not mean you don't/shouldn't present. Rather, it means there's something going on in your psyche—perhaps fear of being judged, perhaps fear of doing badly, etc. That's valuable information for sure, but it's not a red light to your endeavors/responsibilities by any means.

Step 2: Use Emotion as a Clue

Rather than asking, "How do I eliminate this feeling?", ask: "What is it indicating?"

- Anxiety could indicate a fear of getting it wrong.

- Shame could signal a past event that you're carrying forward.

- Resentment could indicate a boundary being overstepped.

Once you decode it, the feeling loses some of its hold, and effectively becomes less of a trap *and more of a map.*

Step 3: Recognize, Then Act Anyway

You don't have to avoid admitting the emotion. You don't have to wait for it to pass either. You can just name it, learn from it, and move on.

Use the mindset:

"Feel it. Learn from it. Don't hand it the steering wheel."

For example, if you feel nervous when writing, tell yourself: "This nervousness means I care. That's helpful—but I'm going to write the opening paragraph anyway."

III: The Micro-Reset: Ground Yourself in the Present

Procrastination often starts in moments when the brain spins out of control—too many thoughts, too much pressure, too many feelings at once. When this happens, you freeze, fidget, scroll, walk away, etc.

It is necessary to have a micro-reset before the spiral takes over. A prompt, practical tool to return your focus to the here and now—so you are able to respond, *not react*.

The objective here is not to psych yourself up. The objective is to reboot your system—*relaxed*, *clear*, and *in-control enough* to take the next step:

Step 1: 4-4-4 Breathing to Reboot the Nervous System

What it is: Inhale for 4 seconds, hold for 4 seconds, exhale for 4 seconds. Repeat a few rounds.

Why it works: Deep inhalations and exhalations instantly suppress the fight-or-flight response and signal the brain that you're safe. This helps you move out of mental fog or panic.

Step 2: Ground Yourself with the "5 Things" Scan

What it is: Silently name 5 things you can see, 4 you can touch, 3 you can hear, 2 you can smell, 1 you can taste.

Why it works: It grounds you in your physical space, taking your focus off of anxious thought patterns. You will slowly feel more present— and less mentally scattered.

Step 3: Tension and Release

What it is: Tense your fists, shoulders, or legs for 5 seconds. Then release. Feel the contrast between tension and relaxation.

Why it works: Physical tension echoes mental pressure. Releasing the physical body sends a message of release back to the brain.

IV: Discomfort Isn't a Signal to Stop

Discomfort shows up fast and loud when you're about to do something challenging. Your brain translates it as a warning: "This doesn't feel right—maybe don't." But that translation is often totally inaccurate.

Discomfort, especially when tasks are involved, doesn't signal danger; it signals that you need to put some effort to jump the hurdle. When you treat it like a red flag, you turn every task into a waiting game.

Here's how to retranslate discomfort as part of the process—not a reason to halt it:

Step 1: Recognize the False Link Between Discomfort and Danger

The human brain, as we've explained in Section 1, is wired to prefer ease. So, when something feels difficult, your mind immediately leaps to: "This must be wrong." But really, all this is, is an outdated safety response. It may have been useful tens of thousands of years ago for our ancestors when survival stakes were very high and the tiniest mistake could well have meant death, but is redundant/useless now.

Recognize that discomfort doesn't mean that you are off track; it often just means that you're doing something that matters, stretches you, or forces focus.

Step 2: Normalize the Friction of Starting

Starting is often the hardest part—not because the task is impossible, or even difficult at all, *but because your brain hasn't shifted gears yet*. That friction is a natural startup cost.

Expect it. Plan for it. *Don't argue with it*.

Think of it like stretching a stiff muscle. It feels tight, not because you're doing damage to it, *but because the muscle is unused and needs warming up and stretching*. A few gentle reps, and it loosens up.

For example, say, you're feeling sluggish prior to cleaning your space and the compulsion to scroll social media kicks in. Rather than give in to the urge, you need to say: "I am only feeling sluggish because I haven't started moving yet. That's normal. I'll simply begin by putting away five things and pick up momentum from there."

Step 3: Act While the Discomfort Is Still Present

Do not wait for comfort to initiate. *Initiate while the discomfort is still present*. Let action come before the emotional shift, *not emotion before the action*.

Even a small step—opening the file, typing one sentence, standing up—begins to build momentum and proves: You can act without feeling completely ready.

V: Create Emotional Space with Self-Distancing Language

When emotion hits hard—stress, anxiety, overwhelm, et al—most of us fall into them all the way in. The language we use betrays this: "I'm stressed out. I'm anxious. I can't concentrate." Complete immersion. And usually once you're in the middle of the storm, it becomes tough to steer.

What needs doing, is to step back and observe the emotion *instead of becoming the emotion*.

This is known as *self-distancing*, and it provides just enough space between you and your feelings to make more effective choices:

Step 1: Switch from "I Am" to "I'm Noticing"

The use of the phrase "I am" fuses your sense of self with the feeling, leading to full emotional immersion.

Practice saying this instead:

- *"I'm noticing anxiety."*
- *"There's frustration here."*
- *"I'm noticing a sense of overwhelm creeping over me."*

This slight change positions you as the observer—*not victim or reactor*.

Step 2: Use the "Part of Me" Tool

Emotions often seem absolute, but they're not. They're fragments; ephemeral moments, *not full definitions of who you are*.

Utilize phrasing like:

- *"Part of me is worried—and that's okay."*
- *"Part of me doesn't want to do this, but another part of me can see that I can/should start small."*
- *"Part of me is scared I'm going to mess this up—and part of me is okay with trying anyway."*

This internal reframe de-cements the grip of the emotion you're grappling with. It separates the feeling from your whole self and allows contradictory truths to coexist.

Step 3: Reframe the Emotion as a Temporary Wave

Feelings pass, especially if you don't attach or resist them.

Use phrases like:

- *"This is just a wave."*
- *"I can ride this without responding."*

This trains your mind to see feelings as *weather*, temporary and bound to pass, and not identity.

VI: Emotional Momentum: Use Movement to Reset State

Emotions don't just live in your head—they run through your entire body. When you're mired in avoidance, hesitation, or fear, it's often not just a mindset issue. *It's typically a state issue*. Your nervous system is stuck in a loop: still body, still mind, stuck feeling.

The reset switch: *change your physical state to change your emotional state*. Motion isn't just physical—it creates emotional momentum as well.

Step 1: Observe Emotional Inertia

Inertia is real—especially emotionally. When you're seated, scrolling, thinking, overthinking… you're still. And stillness tends to feed into the stuck-state and reinforce it.

What helps to be able to get going isn't "thinking better." It's breaking the loop with movement. *Any movement…*

Step 2: Use a Micro-Movement to Break the Loop

Don't wait for motivation. Stand up. Stretch. Walk to another room. Shake out your hands. It doesn't have to be a workout either—it just has to break the stillness.

Here are go-to resets that take less than 2 minutes:

- Stand and stretch for 10 seconds

- Walk to the door and back

- Splash cold water on your face

- Open a window

- Change rooms

These moves signal to your brain: "We're not stuck. We're moving."

Oftentimes when you get back, the task at hand will feel 20% lighter—not because it changed, *but because you did.*

Step 3: Reset the Environment, Not Just the Body

Sometimes your environment anchors your mood. Change the setting, even just for a minute.

Try:

- Switching seats

- Moving your workspace

- Standing instead of sitting

- Turning on a light or music

Small changes send a new response. *New setting, new message.*

For example, if you're feeling drowsy behind the counter of your small business, step away from your post and head out to the shop's outdoor seating area or break room. You might notice that your mind instantly sharpens up – even if just a little – because the fresh setting sends a new cue to your brain.

Now that you understand how to pause and pivot emotionally, you're in a stronger position to *assess and optimize your energy*. Energy is directly tied to emotion, so managing it is the next practical step to avoid slipping back into reactive cycles. The next chapter explores this.

CHAPTER 7

ENERGY > TIME — MANAGING THE RIGHT RESOURCE TO BEAT PROCRASTINATION

"If only I had more time..." This is one of the most common *lies* we tell ourselves when procrastination kicks in. But time is *not* the problem, most of the time—*energy is*. We all get 24 hours, yet some people breeze through grueling days while others can't even get started. Why? Because energy—not time—is truly *the currency of productivity*. Time is finite... limited. Energy, on the other hand, is *flexible*, *renewable*, *manageable* and *stretchable*.

You don't need more hours—you just need more available energy: the mental focus, physical capacity, and emotional space to focus and follow through. This chapter will show you how to boost your energy so that you can actually use your time efficiently and effectively.

Let's get to it.

I: Identify Your Energy Windows, Not Just Your Clock

Time tells you when to work. *Energy tells you how well you will work.*

That's why two people might have the same free hour—but one gets through a project, and another doesn't even get out of the gate. The key difference lies in *energy alignment*, not discipline.

Let's fix that:

Step 1: Observe Your Natural Peaks and Crashes

Start tracking your day—not just by task, but by energy.

For 3–5 days, monitor:

- *When you are intellectually sharp*
- *When you start to flag*
- *When focus comes easily versus when it feels forced*

Don't criticize—just notice and leave it at that. What you're aiming for is to spot patterns, not to criticize yourself.

Here's an example: You may observe that you work most clearly between 9–11 AM, are fuzzy at 2 PM, and have a second wind at 5. Etc.

Step 2: Match Tasks to Energy Type

Not all tasks need the same "kind of brain." So, do not put your most demanding work during your worst hour.

Try this match-up:

- *High-energy windows → creative work, intense concentration, problem-solving*

- *Low-energy windows → admin, routine tasks, email*

- *Crashes/slumps → breaks, walks, resets—not force*

What this is, at its core, is *intelligent task placement*.

Here's an example: You know restocking shelves at 3 PM often feels like a drag. So, you schedule that task for 10 AM, and save simpler stuff – like updating price tags – for the afternoon slump.

Step 3: Organize Around Your Rhythm, Not Against It

Organize your day to ride your waves, not battle them.

- Stack your high-priority task in your peak

- Save low-demand tasks for low-energy times

This approach doesn't just reduce procrastination—it conserves willpower, because *you're not swimming against the current all day*.

Alternative: Instead of starting the day checking voicemails, you jump straight into that tricky customer order or equipment issue – while your mind is at its sharpest. Calls wait until your typical 1 PM lull.

II: Stop Leaking Energy into Decision Fatigue and Clutter

You only have so much mental fuel each day. And much of it is often burned up—not by big obstacles, but by *small, repeated decisions* and a *fog of mental clutter*.

Procrastination often tends to start here—not because a task is too hard, but because your brain is too fatigued to really get going.

Let's plug the leaks:

Step 1: Minimize Small, Repeating Decisions with Pre-Made Routines

Your brain uses energy every single time it has to decide:

> *"What am I supposed to be doing right now?"*
> *"Where do I even begin?"*
> *"Does this have to get done today?"*

Stop deciding in the moment, over and over and over again. Decide once—and let the habit take over, moving forward:

- *Have a morning startup routine (even just 5 minutes will go a long way)*
- *Block out regular times for key task types*
- *Set up your environment in advance*

This removes friction and gets you moving before analysis paralysis occurs.

Here's an example: Rather than figuring out what to do each morning, you simply begin each day by doing 25 minutes of work on your highest priority project – no decisions, no delays.

Step 2: Batch Similar Tasks Together

Constant switching between tasks exhausts attention. Instead, group similar activities together and knock them out in bunches.

- E-mails? Batch them one or two times a day.

- Admin? Set a 30-minute block to get it all done at once.

- Errands? Stack them into a singular window.

Doing this keeps your brain in one mode, which reduces ramp-up fatigue.

Here's an example: Rather than sending and answering messages the moment they come in, you check and respond to everything at 11 AM and 4 PM. The rest of the time stays clean.

Step 3: Create Clear, Visible Next Steps/Actions

Fuzzy tasks are energy and momentum suckers. Your brain keeps going over them, trying to figure out what "get started" even means.

Fix this by:

- *Defining the very next visible step*

- *Putting it on "the visible list" by writing it down or listing it*

- *Keeping your to-do list specific, not general/vague*

For example: Instead of "*Prep for interview*," your list includes: "*List 3 main talking points and open Zoom link.*"

III: Energy Is Affected by What You Consume—Not Just Food

Most of us think of energy in terms of meals, sleep, coffee, et al. But what you take in mentally, emotionally, and physically all day *is every bit as vital to your energy levels*.

If you're feeling constantly tired, spacey, or drained, your energy problem *might be an input problem*.

Let's make that visible—and fixable:

Step 1: Expand Your Definition of "Consumption"

Energy isn't just about calories. You're "consuming" all day long—from food to music to who you talk to.

Split it up into three buckets:

- *Physical inputs: Food, water, sugar, booze, caffeine, exercise*
- *Mental inputs: News, social media, podcasts, YouTube, notifications*
- *Emotional inputs: People, conversations, guilt loops, pressure, criticism*

Every input either recharges or drains your system. Most drains also tend to be silent… insidious—until you crash.

Example: Going through bad/negative news on the scroll during work can make you anxious, and drain your enthusiasm to work, even if you're "just skimming the headlines."

Step 2: Audit Your Energy Inputs

Pick a typical day and ask yourself:

"What am I eating—and how do I feel afterwards?"

Keep this handy checklist handy to track sneaky drains:

Physical:

- *Did I have enough water to drink?*
- *Was my last meal energizing or crashing me?*
- *Am I jittery or crashing due to caffeine?*

Mental:

- *How much time did I burn on reactive material (news, social streams)?*
- *Did I start the day in someone else's world (social media) or my own?*

Emotional:

- *With whom was I interacting—and how did I feel afterwards?*
- *Am I presently mired in guilt, frustration, or comparison?*

Example: After you talk with a specific co-worker, you always feel cranky and disorganized. It helps to recognize that that's not "just the way it is"—that's an energy leak.

Step 3: Reduce, Replace, or Buffer Draining Inputs

Once you have identified what drains you, apply one of three strategies:

- *Reduce: Cut it down/out/Scale it back. Don't start your day on Twitter.*
- *Substitute: Replace with energizing alternatives (e.g., take a few minutes' walk instead of doom-scroll).*
- *Buffer: Buffer with recovery time whenever possible.*

Example: You still need to talk with that energy-draining co-worker—but now you buffer the call up with a 5-minute reset walk to clear your mental space.

IV: Micro-Recovery Beats Heroic Sprints

Ditch the hustle myth, once and for all: grinding out for hours without rest isn't so much productivity as it is *energy mismanagement*. Your brain is not a machine that works better the more it's used. It's a system that runs in cycles—and needs recovery to stay sharp:

Step 1: Get rid of the "Push Through" Mentality

The common belief is: *If I'm not exhausted, I'm not working hard enough*. It's also an incredibly misguided belief seeing as how grinding nonstop only leads to *decision fatigue*, *poor focus*, and *sloppy output*.

Example: If you attempt to pull off a 4-hour work session without breaks, you will most likely end up distracted, mentally foggy, and re-reading the same lines without absorbing anything.

Instead of proving endurance, *start by protecting performance*.

Step 2: Work in Cycles—Not Marathons

Your brain is made for ultradian rhythms—natural cycles of focus that happen approximately 90 to 120 minutes. After that, your performance is bound to flag and suffer.

What works better?

90–120 minutes of focused effort → 5–15 minutes of mindful recovery.

And by 5–15 minutes of mindful recovery, we don't mean an Instagram scroll break. You need to use this time to reset and recharge your system.

Example: After a 90-minute deep clean of the house or workspace, you pause, step outside, stretch your arms, and look at the sky for a few minutes; then you return with a clearer head.

Step 3: Use Simple Recovery Tools

Recovery doesn't need to be complicated. Just change your state. A few ideas:

- *Physical movement: walk around, stretch, move your shoulders*
- *Brief social interaction: say hi to someone, pet your dog*
- *Mental "white space": stare out the window, lie down with eyes closed, breathe*

No input, no stimulation. Just let the brain breathe.

Example: After a deep-focus task, close your eyes and take 10 slow breaths to help you reset for another strong round.

V: Energy Rituals: Build Systems That Replenish Automatically

The best way to protect your energy isn't by waiting until you're drained to recharge; it's by having *small, repeatable rituals* that keep your system steady before it crashes.

Step 1: Switch from Reactive to Proactive

Most people deal with energy slumps after they happen—by reaching for caffeine, taking super long breaks that throw off momentum, or zoning out. *This is reactive, and it's woefully inefficient.*

The shift is this: Don't wait until you're drained. Rather, build small habits that prevent the dip.

Example: Instead of checking your phone first thing and then trying to scramble into focus, you begin each workday with a 3-minute startup/reset ritual that prepares your mind for deep work.

Step 2: Develop a Work-Start Ritual

Your energy isn't a switch that you can flip on command. A short startup ritual primes your brain: "*We're going into focus mode now.*"

Keep it simple and repetitive. Ideas:

- *Clear your desk*
- *Breathe in and out five times*
- *Open your planner and write down one goal for the session*
- *Put on instrumental concentration music*

Step 3: Prioritize Consistency Over Intensity

You don't need long meditations or perfect morning rituals. Small and consistent trumps grand and exceptional.

Start with 1–2 habits that take less than 3 minutes. Anchor them to consistent cues—starting work, finishing a task, coming back from lunch.

Example: Each day, before you unlock the shop or step onto the job site, you pause, close your eyes, and take three deep breaths. Over time, this will become your brain's "start work" cue.

VI: Reinforce Energy Awareness Builds Self-Trust

The more you understand your energy, the less you will have to rely on willpower. Instead of pushing through everything, you begin to work *with* yourself, instead of *against* yourself. That's how you build real momentum—and trust in your own system.

Step 1: Know Your Rhythm, Reduce the Guesswork

When you understand when you work best, when you crash, and what drains your energy, you no longer have to guess what might work.

You no longer wonder: "*Why can't I do this right now?*"

And, instead, start thinking: "*This gets done more effectively at 10 a.m. when I'm alert, not 4 p.m. when I'm fried.*"

Step 2: Rewrite Discipline as Energy Alignment

Discipline is not grinding all the time. It's *getting the right thing done at the right time using the right fuel.*

That's energy alignment, too.

When you're aligned with your energy, showing up becomes easier—not necessarily because you're motivated, but because you're purposeful.

Step 3: Adopt the New Mental Script

Your new script is:

"I don't need to force it. I need to ride the waves."

Energy isn't constant—but it's not random either. With greater awareness, it becomes something you can work with, not against.

To wrap this up, self-trust builds when you stop beating yourself up for not being a machine—*and start respecting your natural flow*. Track your highs and lows. Protect your sources of renewal. Make energy your priority, and you'll find that time begins to take care of itself. *That's how you build discipline that really sticks*.

With your understanding of energy rhythms down pat, you are now ready to structure your day around when you work best. This next chapter shifts the focus from internal regulation to external organization.

CHAPTER 8

DAILY PLANNING THAT WORKS IN REAL LIFE TO BEAT PROCRASTINATION

Most planning systems collapse not because *you* failed—but because they were not built and set up for real life. So, rather than you failing, *they* fail you. Old-fashioned to-do lists, rigid time blocks, and overstuffed, jammed routines tend to collapse the moment something unexpected happens largely *because of design failure*.

To beat procrastination, you don't necessarily need a perfect plan; you just need one that can stretch along with your reality. This chapter explores how to design flexible, low-friction planning habits that can effectively meet you where you are.

Let's get to it.

I: Start with Anchors, Not Ambitions

Most of us start off our days with a long list of what we hope to accomplish. However, ambition-first planning results in frustration once reality fails to collaborate. The more intelligent way of planning is to begin with what is unmovable/inevitable—then structure around it.

Step 1: Identify Your Anchors

Anchors are the essentials/non-negotiables—the things that will happen regardless of whether you schedule them or not. Think meetings, classes, caregiving duties, commutes, regular calls, errands of a fixed duration, etc.

These aren't optional, and they determine the shape of your day whether you acknowledge them or not.

Example: You have a 9–11 a.m. appointment, 3:30 p.m. school pickup, and 6–7 p.m. dinner prep. These are your time anchors. Put them in first.

Step 2: Create a Skeleton Schedule

Once you've set your anchors in place, you've now got a clear visual of your real availability. Note, this is not your "ideal" day… this is your *actual* day. It's that difference that makes the plan work.

This framework reveals the gaps—the available windows in between fixed events. That's where your focus work, family errands, and personal projects go.

Example: With the anchors we laid out in our example in Step 1 in mind, you see you have 11:30 a.m. to 2:30 p.m. free. That's the planning window that you need to work with, and not some hypothetical eight-hour block of productivity.

Step 3: Set the Time You Have Available

Instead of starting with a large list of all the things you'd like to get done and attempting to cram it into an already full day, reverse the approach: ask, "What can be put into the time remaining?"

This approach reduces guilt and overcommitment, because you're *matching tasks to true capacity*.

Example: You've got to service the car, prep dinner, and follow up with a supplier… but you only have 90 minutes. You choose one priority and leave the rest for another day.

Step 4: Ground Your Goals in Reality, Not Fantasy

Planning around anchors grounds you in *what is*, rather than in what "*should be*." It prevents the illusion that you "had the whole day" and prevents you from blaming yourself when things become/feel tight.

II: The Rule of 3: Set a Daily Limit on Major Outcomes

A long task list often feels productive. At least *until it becomes a trap*. When everything is a priority, *nothing is*. This is where the Rule of 3 comes in. It brings focus: Instead of chasing 10 scattered tasks, you identify *just three critical results* that will make your day a success.

Step 1: Define Your "Big 3" for the Day

Your Daily Big 3 are the three outcomes that move the needle. They're not maintenance tasks or small errands; they're those tasks that bring meaning, progress, or closure to the day.

Ask yourself: "*If I only accomplished three things today, what would make the day not be a waste?*"

Example: Rather than a long, sprawling list like:

- Write blog draft

- Respond to 30 emails

- Do laundry

- Watch course videos

- Call plumber

- You narrow it down to:

- Write blog draft

- Submit project proposal

- Follow up with accountant

Step 2: Use the Big 3 to Force Clarity and Priority

This rule *makes* you choose… it forces decisions on your part. You can't do it all—so what's most important? It compels you to separate what's urgent from what's "merely" important, and what's noise from what's genuinely impactful.

When you limit yourself to three, you stop reacting and start to choose.

Example: You may realize that getting your inbox empty isn't as important as completing your budget spreadsheet, even if both are pressing in their own right.

Step 3: Respect Your Attention Bandwidth

Cognitive energy is finite. Chock-full days exhaust you and spread your attention thin. The Rule of 3 maintains your focus, composure, and competence. It conforms to the manner in which your brain truly functions—by conserving energy for what is truly important. For example, instead of darting between fixing a leaky faucet, replying to customers, and half-sorting receipts, *you move with intention through your Big 3*. Even if your day is disrupted, *you know what to come back to and where to pick up from.*

III: Don't List Tasks—List Decisions and Visible Next Steps

A to-do list littered with generalities kills productivity. Writing down "Work on presentation" may look like a plan—but it really isn't. The mind doesn't know where to begin, so it puts it off or works around it.

The way to win is to make your task list *specific*. Here's how to do it: stop the habit of writing down non-actionable tasks and start writing down decisions and specific next steps.

Step 1: Break Abstract Goals into Concrete Moves

When your brain reads "Finish report," it has no clue what that means in the physical sense. Is it outlining? Editing? Sending it? Vagueness breeds avoidance. So instead, grab a pen and put down the first physical thing you can do.

For example, don't write:

"Fix kitchen sink."

Write:

> *"Replace faucet washer and tighten valve."*

That level of specificity converts intention into action.

Step 2: Phrase Tasks as Micro-Decisions

Every task needs to answer the implied question: "*What am I choosing or doing here, exactly?*" This forces specificity. The ambiguity of unclear tasks keeps your mind in limbo. Specificity, on the other hand, gives your mind a clear direction.

Instead of:

> "*Research flights.*"

Try:

> "*Pick travel dates and shop for flights on one site.*"

This way, the task starts with a choice, not just some vague verb.

Step 3: Use Physical Verbs You Can See

The more specific the verb, the easier it is for your brain to follow through. Avoid vague action verbs like "work on," "figure out," or "organize." Use, instead, what you can picture yourself doing: *type, list, send, sketch, rename.*

So:

> *"Sort inventory backlog."*

Becomes:

"*Count and log 5 product categories in Excel.*"

Let's move on to Step 4.

IV: Include a "Buffer Block" for Disruption, Drift, and Delay

Most plans fail not because they were poorly constructed—*but because they assumed nothing would go wrong.* That's never reality.

Life interrupts. Traffic stalls you. A client cancels. Your focus dips mid-afternoon. A simple task takes 4x longer than expected. Etc. When plans leave no margin, even one minor disruption knocks the whole day out of alignment.

That's where a Buffer Block comes in:

Step 1: Acknowledge That Disruptions Are Inevitable

Taking it for granted that your day will roll along without a hitch is pretty much planning for failure. Clever planning ensures to include potential wobbles in the plan.

Think of a Buffer Block as shock absorbers for your schedule. They won't block bumps, *but they keep the whole system from crashing when you bump into one*.

Step 2: Designate a Buffer Block—on Purpose

This is not wasted time… *it's protected space.*

Pick a realistic chunk of your day—usually mid-day or late morning for most of us—where things tend to go sideways and the lull catches up with us. Then, reserve 30 to 60 minutes and leave it free.

You can call it "Catch-up," "Drift Block," or just "Open", and you only use it in case the day starts sliding.

Example:

You needed to run deliveries between 10 and 11, but a vehicle issue eats up 20 minutes. Instead of panicking or abandoning the rest of the route, you know you can shift that portion to a 2:00–2:30 window to stay on track.

Step 3: Reframe Buffers as Strength, Not Slack

Adding buffer time doesn't mean you're going to slack and be lazy—it means *you're going to be resilient*. Planning without margin is gambling. On the other hand, planning with buffers is creating room for real life to happen *without derailing your intention*.

If you don't get a chance to utilize the buffer? That's fine. In fact, *that's ideal*. Just use it to breathe, reboot, or get ahead… that's a win in itself as well.

V: Plan Backwards: End-of-Day Review Before You Begin

Most folks plan out their day in advance in the morning—when hope/optimism is high and memory is foggy. That's how you end up overloading your to-do list or blindly copying yesterday's leftovers without reviewing them.

Intelligent planning doesn't/shouldn't start in the morning. It should start the previous night, *by looking backward before looking ahead.*

Step 1: Ask—What Didn't Get Done?

Before you end the day, scan through your task list for 2 minutes. Don't mindlessly roll over incomplete tasks—ask questions of them.

Ask:

- *"Did this matter?"*
- *"Why didn't I do it?"*
- *"Is it still necessary?"*

Example: You didn't "follow up with supplier." Was it because it's low-priority, or because you need missing order details first? Don't roll it over unless you're sure it's worth the spot.

Doing this prevents your to-do list from being a graveyard of dead intentions.

Step 2: Ask—What Actually Mattered Today?

Sometimes the step/task that made the greatest difference wasn't even on your list.

Perhaps a spontaneous client call created an aha moment. Perhaps sending that quirky email finally cleared mental space.

Ask:

- *"What made the day feel significant or productive?"*
- *"What helped me gain momentum?"*

This redirects tomorrow's priorities—on what *worked*, not what was planned.

Step 3: Ask—What Needs to Be Handled Tomorrow

Now that you've looked back and reviewed, capture reality—not an idealized version of it.

Ask:

- *"What's urgent?"*
- *"What's not complete?"*
- *"What's the one thing I can get in motion?"*

For example, having reviewed, you notice today's avoidance of meeting prep must be tackled early tomorrow morning. You book that in consciously, *rather than remembering in a panic halfway through the morning.*

VI: Use a Simple, Flexible Format You Can Actually Maintain

The perfect system is worthless if you don't use it and stick to it. What actually works is not sophistication; *consistency is what moves the needle.* The perfect planning system is one that you can complete every single day, even on those days when you are tired, rushed, or stressed out.

So, abandon the complicated templates and programs that take 20 minutes of setup time in themselves. Instead, use one of these low-fuss formats that value simplicity over sophistication—and can flex with real life.

Option 1: The 3x3 Grid

This template gives your day structure without bogging it down.

- 3 Big Tasks – The heavy-lifters that will drive/anchor your day.

- 3 Minor Tasks – Lower-intensity tasks like sending an email or making an appointment.

- Minutes of Reflection – A quick end-of-day debrief: What worked? What didn't? What's next?

Example:

Big → Finish slide deck, client call, review proposal

Minor → Respond to Sharon, refill meds, schedule dentist

Reflection → Realized meetings sap more from me than expected; book downtime after next one

This format establishes rhythm and enables you to course-correct in a timely manner.

Option 2: The Sticky Note Plan

Grab a sticky note. That's *all* the space you have for the day.

By limiting how much you can write, you're forced to cut to the core and prioritize. There is no room for filler.

For example:

- Roll out Excel spreadsheet
- Grocery shop

- Email Jeff

- Edit video timestamp 0–3 min

This method is brutally simple—and perfect for hectic days or when mental energy is low.

Option 3: The Time-Box Sketch

Sketch out your day as a rough visual time-plan. Don't aim for perfection/intricate detail... this is not a calendar/journal, after all. Just jot down approximate blocks:

- 9–11 AM: Concentration Work

- 11–1 PM: Errands + lunch

- 2–3 PM: Brief admin

- 3–5 PM: Immersion Work (Proposal)

This method avoids over-blocking and keeps activities grounded in real time, *without rigid scheduling.*

Planning isn't so much about slamming your day into place as it is *about shaping it.* A good plan is something that will adapt, flex, and navigate. Think of it as a practice of everyday calibration, as opposed to a scoreboard. At the end of the day, all you need is a plan that *works*—because you're going to be using it.

Now that daily planning is in place, the next step is learning how to break down and *start* tasks effectively. This helps overcome procrastination's favorite tools: overwhelm and perfectionism. You need to learn to *do* and *ship*, not just plan. The next chapter gets into this.

CHAPTER 9

CHUNK IT, START IT, SHIP IT

One of the biggest procrastination drivers of all is *thinking too big too early*. We get side-tracked by how enormous a task is—so we procrastinate. The solution? *Chunk it*. Break down each project into bite-sized little pieces until the next thing feels almost too easy to ignore. "*Write the report*" becomes "*Jot down 3 bullet points*." "*Clean the apartment*" becomes "*Clear the desk*." Smaller tasks = less friction. That's how you outsmart overwhelm and get things rolling, and this chapter will go into great detail on how to go about it.

Let's get the ball rolling.

I: Use the 10-Minute Rule to Break the Freeze

When you're in that zone of mental fog and paralysis—when even booting up your laptop feels like climbing the Everest—you don't need a master plan or a motivational speech to shake the rust off the wheels. *You just need to get moving*, and that's what the 10-minute rule is for.

The rule is simple:

Tell yourself, "*I will do this for only 10 minutes*." That's it.

Set a timer. Start. Get up and walk away after 10 minutes, *guilt-free*. No need to finish. No need to "trash it." Ten consecutive minutes. *That's all.*

What makes this powerful isn't really the duration so much as the entry point. You're not trying to conquer the whole task; *you're just walking through the door,* at least for now.

Why It Works: The Brain Hates Undefined Starts

Procrastination *thrives in open loops*. If the task is endless or too consequential, your brain puts it off so as not to feel any possible discomfort. But doing only 10 minutes allows your brain a short, safe, easy-to-conquer road. It's no longer "*I must get everything done*." It's "*Let me just do this tiny bit*."

For instance:

- Instead of "*I must write this report*," say, "*I will write the opening two paragraphs for 10 minutes*."

- Instead of "*I need to clean the house*," say, "*I'll tidy the desk for 10 minutes*."

- Instead of "*I have to study*," say, "*I'll review this one concept for 10 minutes*."

Once you're in motion, *momentum takes over*. Often, the hardest part is simply starting. That first keystroke. That first step. That first click.

And here's the incredible thing: Most of the time, you'll just keep rolling, once the handbrake if off. And this won't be because you forced it, but rather because once you're moving, *the psychological resistance wears off.*

The 10-minute rule doesn't guilt you into doing more. It bypasses the resistance and gets you going without an emotional argument. If you stop at 10 minutes, well, that's a win anyway. *You did take control. You did make progress.* And before long, starting will become progressively easier.

Use it daily. *Use it with intention.* And always use it the moment your mind says, "I just can't right now."

Your job isn't to feel ready and perfectly primed before attacking the task. Your job is to simply start—for 10 minutes.

II: Always Define the First Visible Step

To make progress with momentum, and with as little initial resistance as possible, you need to understand and outline what the very first step is. Here's how:

Step 1: Concretize Abstract Goals into Specific Starters

We all tend to write down tasks like "*Study for exam*," "*Work on deck*," or "*Fix website*." The problem with these, is *they don't specify any clear start.*

Zoom in instead:

Ask: *What's my first physical step towards this?*

Examples:

- "Clean the shed"
  → "Sweep one corner and stack the loose tools."

- "Prep for inventory"
  → "Open the checklist and count the top shelf."

- "Fix the truck"
  → "Pop the hood and inspect the battery terminals."

These rewrites give the brain a handle that it can pivot off of, and the clarity reduces resistance and leads to action.

Step 2: Use the 'First Move' Test for Every Task

Before putting a task into your to-do list and getting started with it, perform this mental check:

"If I had to start this task in the next 10 seconds, what would I physically do first?"

If you can't come up with an answer, then *the task is too vague to feasibly start working on.* Break it down until it stands the test.

Example:

- *"Do taxes"* → too big.

  Better: *"Download the W-2 form from email."*

- *"Plan birthday party"* → vague.

  Better: *"Text Mark to confirm the availability of the venue."*

The goal is not to complete it all but to create momentum via specificity.

Step 3: Close Each Session by Creating the Next Starting Point

When closing any work session, take 30 seconds to define how the next one will begin.

Ask yourself: "*What is the next concrete step for future-me to make?*"

Example:

Instead of closing on "*Keep working on report*," leave a sticky note:

"*Next: Open Section 2 and rewrite the first 3 lines.*"

This also decreases the ramp-up friction the next time you sit down.

III: Stack Your Start: Pair the Task with a Starter Cue

Getting started, as we've already highlighted, is often the most challenging part. But what if you could make the start itself automatic—*something your brain instantly recognizes and gets into with less resistance*? That's what starter cues are for.

Step 1: Choose a Consistent Cue That Signals "It's Time"

A starter cue is a small, repeatable action that *acts as a gateway into focused work*. Rather than prioritizing motivation, the starter cue teaches your brain to recognize a pattern.

Examples:

- Put on your work gloves before heading to the garage

- Open the same scheduling app first every morning

- Turn on the same podcast or radio station in the background

- Brew the same morning coffee blend before logging into your system

This cue tells your brain, this is the moment we work.

Step 2: Pair the Cue with the Specific Type of Work

The cue becomes even more powerful when paired with a task of some sort. Over time, the two get linked, *and it becomes easier to get into the flow*.

Example:

- A mechanic may always wipe down their tools before starting diagnostics.

- A shop owner might begin each day by unlocking the register and wiping the counter.

- A freelance photographer may always start by formatting their memory card and adjusting the aperture once before a shoot.

These micro-rituals reduce startup anxiety because *they dispense with the open-endedness of not knowing where to begin*.

Step 3: Keep It Small and Repeatable

Keep it simple. You're not constructing a morning routine—you're cumulatively building up a trigger that puts your brain's "now we work" mode into action.

Consistency is the point, not complexity.

If you consistently:

- Open a specific notebook,

- Wear the same sweatshirt,

- Or crack your knuckles prior to diving in –

Then those things become launchpads for you, with regard to your tasks.

IV: Close the Loop: Finishing Isn't Perfection—It's Progress

Starting is hard—but for most of us, finishing is even harder. The last mile of a project can activate your inner brakes: self-doubt, fear of getting caught, stress about getting it "just right", etc. And that's where momentum quietly perishes.

Let's break that pattern:

Step 1: Recognize Completion Resistance for What It Is

Most of us find ourselves stuck not necessarily at the beginning or even in the middle stages, but at 90% done.

Why? Because completion puts your work out there. It invites criticism. It closes the "doing" chapter and opens up everything you've been working on to scrutiny. That can be very intimidating.

Here are some common indications of completion resistance:

- Tinkering ad infinitum ("Let me just get this one thing right…")

- Abandonment at the eleventh hour

- Procrastination via task-switching

Step 2: Shift the Definition of "Done"

Finished" doesn't have to mean "perfect." Finished only has to mean shipped—submitted, shared, moved forward. Whether perfection/an ultra-high level has been achieved or not *is beside the point*.

Try this mental realignment:

> "*Done means it can be learned from. Perfect means it stays locked inside me.*"

That product sketch? Share it with your team for feedback.

That homemade tutorial video? Upload it – even if the camera angle wasn't perfect.

That service quote? Send it—even if the wording isn't flawless.

Done means the loop is closed, and *closing loops builds confidence*.

Step 3: Build a Practice of "Finishing Ugly

Finishing ugly doesn't mean sacrificing standards. It just means abandoning the expectation *that your work must be flawless to be significant*. Instead, *prioritize momentum over polish*.

For example:

- Get the last paragraph on paper even if it feels clunky—you can fix it later.

- Click "send" on the pitch deck even if one of the charts is not perfect.

- Hit "publish" on the blog post even if the layout isn't quite there yet.

Each finish teaches you something, and that's how progress is made.

Step 4: Use a Completion Cue to Seal the Session

Create a small habit that signals the end of a task:

- Read aloud: "This is finished for today."

- Mark it off your list with purpose.

- Close the file and relocate it to a "done" folder.

This final prompt helps your brain mark closure—which enhances motivation for the next task.

V: Create a "Shipping Mindset" — Push Work Out the Door

Starting requires bravery. Finishing calls for *both bravery and discipline*. Shipping—actually sending your work out there—usually takes an art form of its own. It's not just about the finishing aspect itself... it's about releasing your "baby" to the world and inviting whatever criticisms may come. And that's very, very bold.

Let's build a mindset that doesn't just start and finish—but steels the nerves and ships as well.

Step 1: Practice the Act of "Sending It"

Shipping is a positive action: you send it, publish it, turn it in. It brings the work from inward to outward.

Start to treat these little moments of creation as gym reps. The more you do it, the more you master it:

- Designed a flyer? Print and hang it – don't tweak fonts for two more hours.

- Created a menu draft? Share it – don't wait until it's perfectly styled.

- Prepped a quote for a job? Send it – don't let it sit in limbo.

Every time you ship, you shrink fear and build self-trust.

Step 2: Build the Habit of Finishing and Closing

It's not enough to *almost finish*. The habit we're building involves completely closing the loop outward and actually getting your work out into the world.

Use a personal rule:

> *"If it's 90% done, it's ready to ship."*

Is it rough? Probably. *But nothing teaches faster than feedback from the real world.*

That doesn't happen in your drafts folder.

Step 3: Adopt the "Version Mindset"

Perfectionism whispers: "This better be your best effort."

Version mindset responds: "This is version 1. Let's aim to improve from there."

Think like a programmer. All products start at 1.0, and *the upgrades only come after shipping*. Handle your work the same way:

- This article? Version 1.

- This presentation? Version 1.

- That business idea? Definitely version 1.

When you expect your initial draft to be the final word, you're likely to freeze. But when you leave it open, as a living draft, you're able to flow and execute.

Step 4: Normalize Imperfect Output

The goal is not to get it right, *it's to get it out*.

A useful mantra to lean on:

>   "*If I never ship it, it doesn't exist.*"

That deck you're endlessly polishing and tweaking? No one can benefit from it until it comes off your monitor. That concept you're holding out? It doesn't exist until you ship. Even a rough output creates motion, and motion beats inertia every day of the week.

VI: Let Small Wins Lead the Day

Motivation is not just an internal flame; it's feedback too. One of the fastest, most reliable ways of feeling competent and gaining momentum is by recording what actually got done. *Even if it is only bite-sized.*

If you let small wins guide the day, you're amassing proof that you can start, follow up on, and finish. And that's how momentum is created, rarely ever with hype, and almost always with pure, verifiable facts.

Step 1: Redefine What "Counts" as Progress

We are inclined to discount small actions because they don't feel dramatic enough. But real progress almost always looks like:

- One call placed to schedule the long-overdue appointment.

- One tool cleaned before the next round of work.

- One receipt uploaded that's been lingering in your glove box.

Far from being "minor", these are actually important foundational pieces. Small wins create mental momentum. *You act, you create, you trust.*

Step 2: End Every Session by Logging What You Completed

Instead of wrapping up your day or work session obsessing about what's still on the list, make a short ritual of logging what you actually got done.

Use this simple question:

"What did I finish just now?"

Even if the answer is *"I finally opened the document I've been avoiding,"* it's a win.

Log it.

Step 3: Use Wins to Train Identity, Not Ego

These small actions should not stoke your ego. That's not what their use is. They are meant to be *evidence* builders.

Every time you mark off a task that you've gotten done, you're confirming:

"*I'm a person who completes things.*"

Confidence earned, is what this is. You're not trying to feel good through positive affirmations; you're giving your brain actual data that you're acting and moving forward.

Step 4: Let Completion, Not Size, Be the Metric

It doesn't matter how big the task was – what counts is that it crossed the finish line. You can scale up the scope later. For now:

- Sent that job estimate?

- Cleared one small section of the garage?

- Drafted a rough bullet list for the new signage?

Each of these wins trains your nervous system *to associate action with relief—not fear*.

The primary point of this chapter is to not worry about the finish but rather, to *focus on the step that initiates it*. Chunk it. Start it. Ship it. Aim to get moving, because small victories stack up fast.

After learning how to break down big tasks, start quickly, and finish without over-polishing, you are most certainly, at this point, empowered to take more action—but even the best momentum can get derailed by stress, fatigue, or sudden overwhelm. That's where the **30-Minute Reset Routine** comes in. This routine offers a *structured, repeatable* system to recover clarity and direction when things go sideways, which will help ensure that action doesn't stall for long and that forward movement can always be rebooted. The next chapter explores this.

CHAPTER 10

THE 30-MINUTE RESET ROUTINE TO REGAIN CONTROL WHEN YOUR DAY IS SLIPPING

When we're feeling fuzzy-headed, disorganized, or lagging behind, most of us instinctively default to two responses: *push harder or collapse*. Neither works very well. What you need is actually a Reset Routine; a low-stress, judgement-free system to *pause, clear your head,* and *come back in with intention*. This reproducible, real-world mechanism will enable you, time and time again, to shift gears and get back in the groove, no matter how far you've strayed.

Let's get to it.

Step 1 (Minutes 0–5): Pause, Breathe, Unload

When your day starts to get away from you – tasks piling up, thoughts whirling, etc. – the last thing you need to do is attempt to push through in a panic. Step one shouldn't include doing something/anything. *Interruption* should be the first step.

Before you try to "solve" anything, you have to interrupt and pause the internal turmoil. This step has nothing to do with mood or meditation. Rather, it is purely tethered to grabbing and steeling the mental wheel before it steers off into madness.

Action 1: Sit Still and Interrupt the Noise.

Sit down. Plant your feet on the ground. Put on a 2-minute timer. Then, breathe.

- No mindfulness ceremonies or deep breathing needed.
- Just slowly breathe in through your nose and out through your mouth.
- Four seconds in, four seconds out.

You're not relaxing… you're *breaking the pattern*; initiating a hard reset to the head storm.

Example: You're at the middle of your workday, tab-switching between different things, mid-task task-swapping, etc. So, you pause. The two minutes or so of slow breathing that you perform should help drop your heart rate and coax you back from the abyss of autopilot.

Action 2: Fast Mental Unload

Next, grab a notepad, phone, or scrap paper. Set a 3-minute timer. Write down everything that's whirling around in your mind.

Don't sort and don't filter. *Just dump.*

- "Email boss"
- "Buy detergent"

- "I'm falling behind again"
- "Why am I this way?"

Let it be mixed up and messy. Clarity isn't what we're after here; *extraction* is.

Example: You catch yourself in analysis paralysis. So, you breathe, and you brain-dump 17 disjointed thoughts on a page. Now, what was previously only a mess in your mind is now ink on paper. *Physical. Organizable.*

Why This Works

When your mind is overloaded, it's trying to hold everything in working memory at the same time. And that's just not feasible. By breathing and externalizing the chatter, you are able to actively make room so that your nervous system can unwind, and your mind is able to regain traction.

Step 2 (Minutes 5–10): Reconnect with Your Current State

Once you have unloaded the clutter in your mind, you have cleared the desk; however, you must now find out *what's really going on beneath the surface*. You're not trying to cure yourself so much as you're trying to get real with what's happening inside you, *right now*.

Action: Ask Yourself These 3 Questions

Set the timer to 5 minutes. Write down rapid, honest answers – a few words or a phrase at most. No censoring, and no editing.

1. What's the real truth on why I feel stuck right now?

Don't default to "I'm lazy" or "I'm behind." Drill one layer deeper.

Example: *"I feel stuck because I'm not sure which part of the engine to inspect first."*

Example: *"I'm hesitating because I feel awkward calling the client back without all the info."*

Precision is the goal here.

2. What emotion or sensation is dominating my system?

Skip wishy-washy label words like "off" or "meh." Use words describing the emotional or physical state.

Example: *"My chest is tight and I'm anxious"*

Example: *"I'm clenching my jaw and irritated"*

Example: *"I'm spaced out and heavy"*

Labeling defuses intensity; it takes you out of suffocating in the feeling, and into observing it from a more neutral base.

3. What would get me one notch more competent or in control?

Not a whole solution. Just one notch better. Think small.

Example: *"Putting my phone on silent would help."*

Example: *"Clearing this workbench and grabbing the wrench would help."*

Example: *"Turning on the fan and setting a 15-minute timer would help."*

This question drops you into a micro-sense of agency, from helplessness. And that's the nook where traction begins.

Why This Matters

You can't change direction if you don't know where you stand a present. This step gives you emotional GPS—quick and genuine calibration *without rumination*.

Step 3 (Minutes 10–15): Clean or Tidy One Physical Zone

Now that you've cleared your mind and checked in with yourself, it's time to get your body involved. Again, the goal here isn't productivity… it's momentum. You're using *light*, *intentional* movement to reset your state and reclaim a sense of control.

Action: Spend 5 Minutes Tending to One Small, Visible Space

Choose one zone – something that's in your physical environment and within reach.

- A cluttered tool shelf or workbench

- The driver's seat of your car or van

- A pile of receipts or paperwork on your counter

- Your digital clutter: messaging apps, booking calendar, camera roll

Set a timer for 5 minutes only.

Examples of what to Do in That Time

- Stack papers

- Discard trash

- Clean a surface

- Close unnecessary tabs

- Archive or delete 10 emails
- Fold two items and discard one

The aim here is *noticeable progress*.

Example: "*I cleared off one side of the workbench—I can finally lay my tools flat.*"

Example: "*I closed 12 open service requests and now my screen feels breathable.*"

Example: "*I emptied my glove box and finally found the spare keys. Small win.*"

Why This Works

Visual order sends a powerful message to your brain:

> "*I'm in control. I can manage my world.*"

When the mind is mentally cluttered, small physical wins help to break through the chaos. You don't really need to psych yourself up; you just need to move something from a state of disorganization to one of order. That sensory shift anchors you and builds quiet momentum.

Step 4 (Minutes 15–20): Check in on Today's Original Intention

Now that you've cleared your head, grounded your body, and taken out a bit of chaos from your environment, *it's time to re-orient.*

This does not mean reconstructing the whole day... the aim here is to identify the one solid thread you need to return to: your initial intention.

Action: Revisit the Day's Purpose

Start by asking:

> "*What was today supposed to be about?*"

If you have a plan in advance, pull it out. Look at your calendar, notebook, task list, or app.

Otherwise, just bring the initial mindset you had in the morning to the fore:

- What did you expect to happen today?
- What did you hope to get done cr make progress on?

Example: "*I planned to get that report outlined.*"

Example: "*I wanted to get some progress made on cleaning the apartment.*"

Example: "*I had three follow-up calls that I was going to make.*"

Now: Assess the Current Reality

Check the time. Take stock of your energy now. Be honest.

Ask yourself:

- Is the original plan I had in mind realistic at this point?
- Did something change that resets today's top priority?

  Example: "*I lost two hours to an unexpected walk-in client – finishing the full product batch today isn't realistic.*"

Example: *"I'm more exhausted than I anticipated, but I still have it in me for one follow-up call."*

Recommit to One Anchoring Intention

Do not go after the whole to-do list. Do not try to "catch up on lost time."

Instead, look to get reconnected to one meaningful action or theme that gives integrity to the day.

> *"Today is now about placing that key parts order."*

> *"It's about giving 30 minutes of focused time to the main repair job."*

> *"It's about completing one clear, hands-on task that moves things forward."*

That is your new anchor.

Step 5 (Minutes 20–25): Reframe the Next Move

Now that you've re-integrated your day's purpose, the next thing to do is to *not* charge at your entire to-do list. *That would only revisit the overwhelm that derailed you in the first place.*

Instead, you zoom in. Big time.

Rather than trying to "get back on track", the goal here is to choose one completable, forward step to get your momentum rolling.

Action: Find Your "Restart Step"

Ask yourself one of the following questions:

- *"What's something I can do immediately that gets me in motion?"*

- *"What would winning, in 5 minutes, look like?"*

- *"What's the thinnest sliver of progress I can physically complete?"*

Example: You had "revised the whole report" on your step list. Restart step: open the file and edit the first paragraph.

Example: You wanted to "sort finances." Restart step: verify one account balance.

Example: You wanted to "apply to 3 jobs." Restart step: update contact information on your resume.

Why It Works: Momentum Beats Motivation

Your brain is looking for frictionless re-entry – not master plans.

When you choose a task that:

- is concrete

- can be accomplished in under 10 minutes

- had a tangible completion…

…it circumvents resistance and initiates motion.

A little triumph – even sending one email, getting rid of 5 junk files, or assigning a name to a file – can automatically shift your state from "stuck" to "in motion."

Step 6 (Minutes 25–30): Begin That One Action – Right Now

This is where reset becomes reality.

You've cleaned out mental mess, reconnected with your purpose, and chosen a small Restart Step.

Now, you act.

Not after one more scroll. Not after making it a little bit more perfect.

You act *now*.

Action: Set a 5-Minute Timer and Begin

Whatever your Restart Step was – start doing it now, *for just 5 minutes*.

Set a physical timer if needed.

No conditions. No perfection.

The job *is to begin*, not finish.

Example: If your Restart Step was *"reorganize the tool rack,"* just start by grouping the wrenches.

Example: If it was *"clear the front counter,"* start with the paperwork on the left.

Example: If it was *"follow up with the supplier,"* just open the email and type out the greeting.

Why This Works: Action Rewires State

You're not trying to think your way out of being stuck anymore... you're giving your brain some physical evidence that motion is possible, even if it doesn't feel like it.

This short burst flips the switch from "frozen" to "engaged."

Also, how long you go past the timer is neither here nor there.

The 5 minutes are the win.

Optional Wrap-Up: Build the Pattern

When the 5 minutes are up:

- Record what you've done ("*Cleaned top shelf*," "*Replied to 4 customer texts*," etc.)

- Briefly check in with how you're feeling now compared to 30 minutes ago

Doing this closes the loop. It also programs your mind to *link being stuck with productive resets, not spirals*.

Small changes, done repeatedly, become habits, and these habits, when practiced long enough, eventually *become your new normal*.

To wrap it up, a Reset Routine has very little to do with damage control. A Reset Routine is *something that you can do at any point to shift gears intentionally*. The more you do it, the faster you bounce back. As such, it is imperative that you don't waste energy trying to "catch up." Just reset. Re-enter. Then, move ahead. This is what making progress is all about.

Now that you have a practical routine to recover from overwhelm, the next step is to learn how to *prevent* that overwhelm by controlling incoming noise – emails, notifications, advice overload, etc. Cluttered input = scattered output. The next chapter explores this.

CHAPTER 11

CLEAR THE INPUT CLUTTER

A ll too often, procrastination, as opposed to stemming from outright avoidance, is the by-product of *too much mental traffic*. Input clutter – emails, headlines, alerts, tabs, group chats, you name it – all of these create constant cognitive load that steadily de-psyches you from buckling down and actually attacking your task(s). When your brain's "inbox" is full, it becomes very hard to sustain clarity, which leads to assertive action predictably stalling. This chapter explores how to filter and manage inputs, and, in so doing, eliminate decision paralysis.

Let's get the ball rolling.

I: Identify Your Default Intake Channels

Rule number 1 when it comes to management: *You can't manage that which you haven't identified.*

So that you have a clear understanding on what it is; input clutter is the accumulation of unfiltered, unsorted, and relentless "incoming" – *digital*, *mental*, and *physical*. When that noise piles up, it leads to mental drag. You're focused *but unfocused…* alert *but perpetually diverted*.

You have to know where input clutter is entering your system before you can reduce it.

Let's map that out:

Step 1: Scan Your Digital Intake

Start with the obvious culprits: your screens.

Ask yourself:

- What apps or sites do I habitually check?
- Where do I get coaxed and pulled into chats or notifications that I didn't specifically ask for?
- Look at the following:
- Multiple client communication channels (texts, voicemails, app notifications)
- Group chats for family, staff, or teams
- Job management apps or service request dashboards
- Tools, tabs, or devices running in the background
- Notifications from payment apps, delivery trackers, or scheduling tools

Example: You realize that you check three different inboxes – plus WhatsApp, Telegram, and Instagram – all within 10 minutes of waking up. That's *six* input gates *before your day has even started.* That's just way too much, especially right out the gate.

Which leads us to this…

Step 2: Surface Your Mental Intake Channels

Your mental intake channels are the abstract "to-remembers" and "should-checks" that constantly wander through your mind:

- Random reminders like "I need to book that appointment"

- Ideas you meant to jot down but didn't

- Suddenly-recalled loose threads from undone/half-finished tasks

Example: You repeatedly find yourself thinking, "*I should read that article*" or "*Don't forget to call Sarah,*" but never get them down on paper. They loop through your brain over and over again, *taking up valuable bandwidth.*

Step 3: Walk Through Your Physical Intake Points

Survey your workspace—or wherever you have the tendency to "drop" things.

Physical input channels typically include:

- Stacks of unopened mail or flyers sitting by the entryway

- Scribbled notes on a whiteboard or shop counter

- Spiral notebooks with scattered to-do items

- Unsorted parts, supplies, or inventory boxes

- Receipts or forms you meant to file "later"

For example: Your workspace holds 12 sticky notes, three books left open, and an "URGENT" tray of papers that has been sitting pretty for over a week. Best believe that each one pulls at your attention – even passively.

Step 4: Do a Quick Intake Audit

Now that you've pinpointed your sources of intake in your digital, mental, and physical spaces, you need to answer one key question:

"Where is most of my incoming noise actually coming from?"

You might find that:

- 80% of your stress comes from client calls scattered across platforms

- Or it's the 5 devices or dashboards you're toggling between

- Or it's the pile of unprocessed notes you carry from job to job

Awareness is the win here. If you know your inputs, then you can begin to control and filter them *instead of being controlled by them.*

This is where input management starts; not necessarily in deletion or detoxing, but in *clear awareness of the flow*. The next steps get into this.

II: Create an "Incoming Gatekeeper" Rule

Your attention isn't a public park. Not everything can/should get in.

Too many of us live in "default-on" mode: every email lands in the inbox; every notification pings; every app stays running; every group chat is allowed to claw at our attention, etc.

The issue with this, is that sustained attention and lowered cognitive load call for the polar opposite: A framework that treats attention *as a scarce resource*, boxed in by a Gatekeeper Rule.

Step 1: Adopt a "Default-Off" Attitude

Start with this attitude shift

Nothing warrants your attention on autopilot. *It has to earn its spot.*

Before letting any input come in – email sign-up, group, app, alert, conversation, et al – ask:

> *"Does this consistently drive me forward, or does it mostly just take space?"*

If the answer is not a straight up, loud yes, opt out immediately.

The Gatekeeper Rule here is quite simple: *Only opt in if it delivers recurring value.*

Step 2: Use the "3-Strike" Rule for Subscriptions

Automate your filter by having a clear cutoff:

- If you delete a newsletter 3 times in a row, unsubscribe.

- If a podcast is left un-listened to for a month, remove it from your feed.

- If a YouTube channel is more distraction than direction, unfollow.

Step 3: Mute or Leave Non-Essential Group Threads

Group chats can be beneficial. A lot of the time, however, they often just devolve to becoming input firehoses.

Set a simple boundary:

- *Mute any thread that is not connected to a current goal or relationship that matters.*

- *Leave discussions that are mainly noise or memes unless they have a clear emotional/social benefit.*

Step 4: Use "One-Tab Browsing" and a Read-Later List

Too many tabs = distracted attention.

Instead:

- Have one open browser tab when doing deep work.

- Consume articles, videos, and ideas from a read-later app (e.g., Pocket or a plain Notion list).

- Take an hour each week to browse your backlog, or just delete it, guilt-free.

III: Create a Clean Capture System

It's very difficult to focus if your brain is trying to remember 43 unrelated things at once. Procrastination often spikes because your mental RAM is maxed out. Thoughts, reminders, random ideas, obligations, and worries, etc. all take up a slice of your mental RAM. The other thing is that the vast majority of that noise isn't really about what you're doing – *it's about what you're trying not to forget.*

The fix here isn't more memory (not that this is even really feasible, with regard to the brain.) The fix is *a clean capture system*.

Step 1: Distinguish Between Input Clutter and Captured Info

There is a vast difference between input clutter and captured information.

- Input clutter: Stuff zinging at you (text, thought, tasks, ideas, et al) with no system to confine them.

- Captured info: The very same stuff, but this time *logged and externalized*, so your mind knows it's taken care of.

Example: You're repairing a fence and suddenly remember that you need to call the hardware supplier. Without a capture system, that thought loops in your head until it becomes a real distraction – or pulls you off-task entirely.

With a capture system, you merely jot down "Buy bulbs" in your notes and go on.

Step 2: Choose One Central Capture Tool

It does not matter what you choose to use. What matters is that it is *consistent*, *central*, and *trustworthy*.

Pick one of the following:

- A pocket notebook

- A specialized notes application (like Apple Notes, Google Keep, Notion)

- A continuous text file or digital notepad on your computer

This will be your "inbox for the mind" – where all new ideas, reminders, thoughts, and tasks land first.

Step 3: Log Everything *Immediately* (No Sorting Yet)

Avoid the trap of "I'll organize this later" before capturing.

- Don't categorize it.

- Don't decide when to do it.

- Just get it out of your head.

Example: You're at lunch and you think of a sentence you might put in your client pitch to make it even punchier. You shouldn't wait to set up a new folder for "client ideas" so you can log it there – you stick it right into your single capture point immediately.

The organization will come later.

Step 4: Review the System at a Set Time

Captured clutter only stays "clean" if you get through it regularly.

Apply one simple habit:

> "*I review my capture system at least once a day.*"

When you review, you:

- Clear away what doesn't matter

- Convert ideas to tasks or calendar spots

- Put anything important where it goes (project folder, email, calendar, etc.)

The magic in doing this, is this: your brain starts to trust that it *doesn't* have to remember everything, which means it can now focus, undistracted.

Step 5: Treat Your System as a Mental Inbox, Not a Junk Drawer

Everything gets in – but everything gets dealt with and processed too.

No drawn-out build-up, no random Post-Its, and most certainly no having ten open apps at a time.

IV: Set Clear Input Boundaries in Time, Not Just Tools

You might have inbox zero and the perfect note-taking app, but if you're constantly checking email, social streams, and chat threads, your mind never gets the chance to truly go deep. The point here is that it's not enough to clean your tools – you must manage when they get access to your time, too.

That means setting *time-based boundaries* for your inputs—not just tool-based ones.

Step 1: Recognize the Hidden Problem: 24/7 Access Means Zero Recovery

Most of us don't realize that we're plugged into input mode *all day long*.

We scroll while eating, check email "just for a second" between tasks, get pinged by notifications mid-flow, read headlines before you've even gotten out of bed, etc.

Even if the inputs are useful, the constant timing creates two problems:

- Your brain never exits reactive mode

- You sacrifice execution for endless intake

Step 2: Define Specific Time Windows for High-Noise Inputs

You don't have to cut out all inputs… you just need to *keep them in line*.

Choose clear, reasonable windows to check high-noise sources like:

- Voicemail and text messages

- Order tracking systems

- Service dashboard

- Group chats or team check-ins

Then stick to the principle: no access outside those windows.

Example: You set your rule: "Messages and updates at 11 a.m. and 4 p.m. Not before and not in between." Everything else waits.

This helps create mental boundaries that your brain can rely on: rest when off, work fully when on.

Step 3: Turn Off Passive Notifications During Concentration Blocks

Most inputs do not come because you seek them.

They come because they interrupt you.

As such, you need to create "areas of shielded execution" by turning off:

- Phone alerts (apart from emergency contacts)
- Desktop alerts (calendar reminders, Slack popups)
- Background email notifications

Example: Before beginning a critical equipment repair, first silence notifications, put your phone in a drawer, and close the service app dashboard – so that the 90-minute block you've set aside stays focused and interruption-free.

Step 4: Anchor Input Rules to Specific Events

Make your boundaries easy to maintain by associating them with events or routines.

Use such anchors as:

- *"I don't check news until after lunch."*
- *"I only respond to messages after my focused work block."*
- *"I only scroll during dog walking."*

Having rules anchor to habits reduces decision fatigue and pins the habit into your psyche.

Step 5: Defend the Output Hours by Treating/Guarding Them Like Meetings

You would not take a random some telephone call during a client meeting now, would you? Treat your creation/output times in the same way.

Mark them out on your calendar and, if feasible, tell coworkers, family, or teammates that those are your off-input zones.

Example: 9am–11am, you write. Phone on silent. No apps and no inputs so that your mind has an uninhibited runway to attack the work.

V: Prune, Archive, or Eliminate: Perform a Weekly Input Cleanse

Digital inputs tend to pile up stealthily. Tabs multiply, notes accumulate, the inbox count rises, etc. And even if you're actively managing your attention throughout the week, this digital detritus creates drag, both mental and emotional, so that every unclosed loop keeps whispering "You need to deal with me."

A simple fix for this, is having a weekly input purge.

Step 1: Clear the Tabs (All of Them)

You don't need 29 tabs open. Let's be honest, you're not going back to half of them.

Perform a tab purge on a weekly basis:

- Close everything not in active use

- If you'll possibly need to go back to something, save it to a reading list or note app

- Bonus: Use a browser extension that auto-saves session tabs upon close, if you're worried

Step 2: Archive and Sweep Notes

That idea you wrote down three days ago? It's either gold, or it's noise.

Spend five minutes:

- Moving valuable notes into their rightful place (a folder, a project file, etc.)

- Erasing spontaneous snaps no longer relevant to you

- Tagging or batching anything still "in progress" so it won't disappear

Step 3: Clear the Digital Inbox Backlog

Whatever it is – email, saved items, unread feeds, or open threads – pick one input backlog to zero out.

You don't need to reply to all of it. You just need to decide what's left open and what isn't.

Tactics:

- Unsubscribe from anything you've been avoiding reading 3 times in a row

- Batch archive anything over a week old unless time-sensitive

- Highlight only 2–3 follow-ups for next week

Step 4: Eliminate or Mute Input Channels That No Longer Serve You

A channel is only worth it if it serves your intentions or purpose.

Every week, review your open input channels:

- Group chats

- Slack channels

- Feeds

- Notifications

Ask: "*Is it useful—or just noise masquerading as relevance?*"

Then, mute, leave, or delete *without guilt*.

Step 5: Use Filters or Folders to Streamline Recurring Inputs

If you're keeping some inputs, put them in line.

Set Up:

- A "Read Later" folder for newsletters

- Filters that skirt your main inbox

- A weekly digest folder for low-priority updates

This keeps regular input out of mind until it's time to deal with it.

For example, you can create a Gmail filter so all newsletters skip the inbox and go into a "Newsletters" label. Then, you may check that folder once a week, *on your terms*.

To wrap it up, less input isn't so much shutting down stimulation as it is *filtering what is important enough to deserve your attention*. Cutting through the noise ekes out vital space for clarity, better decision making, and laser-focused action. You'll *think faster*, *feel more unencumbered*, and *get more done*.

Once readers learn how to cut through the noise and reduce external clutter—notifications, advice, constant input—they're left with a quieter mental space. But silence often brings clarity *only if* we know where to look. That's where **Zoom Out** comes in. With distractions minimized, this chapter helps readers lift their head from the day-to-day grind and reconnect with the bigger picture, giving them direction and renewed perspective when they feel mentally jammed.

CHAPTER 12

ZOOM OUT — REGAIN PERSPECTIVE WHEN YOU'RE STUCK

Sometimes, the reason why you feel (and are) stuck is because you're so deep in the weeds – so focused on details and what not – that it *takes your focus away from the main purpose*. When the focus lens narrows too much, clarity tends to dissolve, which ultimately leaves you unable to leave square one. This chapter focuses on lifting your perspective so that it fixates on the big picture, and so that you can finally get the handbrake off and get rolling.

Let's get started.

I: The Altitude Ladder: Move Up a Level, Mentally

Often when we're stuck, it's because our attention is trapped at a singular level of thinking. For example, you're sweating over a line in an email, a sentence in a chapter, or a detail in a plan, etc. and nothing's moving as a result.

This is the time to zoom out.

Think of mental perspective as an altitude ladder. There are five rungs:

1. *Task-level — The exact thing you're doing*

2. *Project-level — The broader work it belongs to*

3. *Goal-level — What you're trying to accomplish*

4. *Identity-level — Who you're becoming*

5. *Life-level — What's going on season-wise, and what matters in the present*

Each level gives you a different kind of clarity. If one isn't paying off, you need to promptly shift to the next, and so on.

Step 1: Determine Where You're Currently Stuck

Ask: *What level am I struggling with now?*

Example: You can't decide which wrench to use for a repair. That's task-level.

Knowing at what level you are at makes you understand what kind of clarity you're seeking, *and what kind you might be missing.*

Step 2: Move Up One Level

Now ask: What's one level higher—and what does it explain/clarify?

- From task → project: "What is this section meant to accomplish?"

- From project → goal: "Why does this article matter?"

- From goal → identity: "What kind of writer am I attempting to be?"

- From identity → life: "Given my priorities right now, how important is it that this comes out flawless?"

Each shift provides breathing room; it interrupts the cycle of over-focusing and *reconnects the task to a broader meaning.*

Example: Instead of agonizing over which invoice template looks most professional (task), you remind yourself: I'm building a habit of treating this side hustle seriously (identity).

Step 3: Choose Action from the Higher Level

Having zoomed out, return to the task with guidance from above, pun intended.

"If the point of the repair checklist is to ensure safety and accuracy (project-level), then it doesn't need to be perfectly worded; just clearly actionable will do."

II: Create a Personal Zoom-Out Prompt

If you're mired deep in frustration, resistance, or single-minded focus on one thing, then you're really not seeing the larger picture that's supposed to give your actions their significance. Think of it like trying to find your way somewhere by tracking one blade of grass at a time.

Zooming out isn't automatic – it's a skill that you can tap into by design. And it starts with one question.

Let's build yours.

Step 1: Choose a "Purpose Prompt" That Reminds You of the Why

This is the question that gets you out of task tunnel vision and reminds you of why you started it in the first place.

Try:

- "What's the bigger purpose here?"

- "What is this task supposed to serve?"

- "How is this connecting to something that actually matters to me?"

Example: You're rewriting a customer message for the fifth time. You ask yourself, "What's the goal here?" You then remember: It's to confirm the appointment – not craft the perfect sentence. That clarity helps you move forward.

Choose one prompt that feels true to you and keep it handy.

Step 2: Add a "Problem Reframe" Prompt That Disrupts Over-Identification

This prompt helps you step back and detach yourself from the emotional noise and turbulence of the moment.

Try:

- *"If this problem weren't here, what would I be focusing on?"*

- *"Am I reacting to the task, or the story I'm telling about it?"*

- *"Is there another reason for this tension?"*

Step 3: Use a Future Lens Prompt to Regain Perspective

A simple, quick time-shift can shrink the moment's magnitude.

Try:

- *"How will I view this one month from now?"*
- *"Will this even matter next week?"*
- *"What would future-me thank me for doing right now?"*

Step 4: Save and Use Your Personal Zoom-Out Set

Select one question from each of the three categories – Purpose, Problem, and Future. List them. Then, carry this list with you as a "reset card" whenever you feel overwhelmed, stuck, or disconnected. Whenever you leverage this reset card, it will help you regain enough mental altitude to progress from scattered reaction to grounded action.

III: Story Check (Rewrite the Internal Narrative)

When you're stuck, you're rarely ever just battling a task – a lot of the time, you're also *battling the story you're telling yourself about the task.*

This is often unconscious and automatic:

- *"I'm behind."*
- *"This shouldn't be this hard."*
- *"If this part's not working, then everything is falling apart."*

These narratives shrink your mental space, which creates tunnel vision, not clarity.

The fix for this, is to interrupt the scroll and then rewrite it:

Step 1: Spot the Current Story Playing in the Background

Before you try to power through the resistance, put a tag on what you're already telling yourself about this situation.

Ask yourself:

"What's the internal headline I'm believing right now?"

It might be:

- *"This isn't going well."*
- *"I should've received this by now."*
- *"Everything rides on getting this just right."*

This is important because once you get to see the story, you can finally stop living inside it and begin editing it.

Step 2: Generate Three Alternate Narratives

Now, re-write the scroll. Ask yourself:

"What are three other realistic, valid stories that can explain this moment?"

The idea here is not to try and fool yourself; you're trying to take a step back and create options.

Examples:

- *"This might just be a normal plateau that comes right before clarity."*

- *"Maybe the task is a tad off-kilter from how I work best."*

- *"This might be a signal I need a break, feedback, or a quick reboot, not a signal that I'm failing."*

When you have multiple narratives, your mind stops dwelling and locking in on just one, and you're able to regain your agency.

Step 3: Choose the Story That Motivates You

Choose the story that is honest and useful. You don't even need to believe it 100%. You just need one that allows you to move one step forward with less resistance.

For example:

> *"This bit is hard, but I am genuinely learning something from it. Let's try one small move and see how that pans out."*

IV: Revisit the Why: Realign with the Original Intention

When progress stalls or frustration builds, a lot of the time it's because the task has detached from its purpose... you're no longer writing to communicate something important – you're just trying to "finish the damn slide." And when this happens, then you're not building toward growth anymore... you're just trying not to fall behind.

This is the perfect time to zoom out and *realign with your original why*:

Step 1: Ask the Anchor Question

Pause and ask yourself:

"What was this work for? What is it supposed to be in service of?"

Not the task itself, *but the reason behind it.*

Was it...

- Freedom?
- Growth?
- Contribution?
- Learning?
- Completion?

For example:

You didn't start drafting the service estimate to impress the client with technical jargon. You wanted to clearly present pricing and help them decide. *That's your actual why.*

Step 2: Check for Alignment Drift

Now ask:

"Is how I'm working right now consistent with that initial intention?"

This puts the moment back into context and, subsequently, helps you answer this question: "Am I stuck because the work has lost its connection to my motivation?"

If, for example, your "why" was learning, but you're now obsessing about getting it "right," then you've lost your direction. If your "why" was freedom, but your current process/approach feels like a trap, then likewise, something is wrong.

Step 3: Make One Micro-Adjustment Towards the Why

Realignment does not require completely reorganizing the task. It simply needs to be pushed back in the direction of intent.

- If the "why" was growth → *Add a step of reflection at the end.*

- If the "why" was contribution → *Ask, "Who will this serve?":*

- If the "why" was completion → *Establish a finish line for today.*

One small adjustment can (and will) bring you back into alignment with the true purpose, which will help unleash your momentum.

V: Pull Back the Time Frame: Zoom Out on the Timeline

Task paralysis thrives in the zoomed-in, close-up perspective.

If all you can see is the short-term roadblock – the missed deadlines, the messy draft, the lagging motivation, et al – then it is bound to feel like everything is falling apart. Nonetheless, perspective isn't all about goals; it's about the timeline too, which leads us to this: you don't necessarily need a creative strategy, *you just need a wider lens.*

Here's how to shift your timeframe and ease up the negative emotional energy that causes you to stall:

Step 1: Ask Where You Are in the Larger Arc

Zoom out from "now" to the whole journey. Ask yourself:

- *"Where am I in the big picture of this project?"*

- *"Am I starting, middle, or finishing?"*
- *"Have I done this before and gotten past it?"*

Example: You're halfway through repainting your shop and starting to feel fried. But when you stop and reflect, you realize this dip often always happens mid-project. If you just keep moving forward, momentum always returns. That insight alone brings relief.

Name the phase and normalize the feeling.

Step 2: Look Back Three Months

Reflecting back on where you were 90 days prior will reconfigure your sense of momentum.

Reflect on the following:

- *"Things were tough back then. So, what exactly was I fighting?"*
- *"What have I accomplished, even if progress initially seemed slow?"*
- *"What do I understand differently or manage more effectively?"*

Step 3: Look Six Months Down the Road

Now flip the lens forward. Ask:

- *"What do I want to have fixed or built by then?"*
- *"Will today's frustration even register at that scale?"*
- *"What small step today moves me in that direction?"*

Example: Say, you're agonizing over/grumbling about an off day. Look six months down the road – after you've submitted the project, established the habit, or made the switch – and try to determine if today's slump will either be a footnote or a headline by then (the former will be a lot likelier.)

Leveraging the long view makes today's discomfort seem a lot smaller.

Step 4: Name This Moment for What It Is

Don't dramatize where you're at… define it and leave it at that.

Is this a:

- Temporary dip?
- Signpost for rest?
- A normal creative plateau?

Labelling the moment can stop you from turning an interim phase into a permanent identity.

VI: Choose the Next Best Step from a High-Altitude View

Zooming out is only half the fight.

Once you've reignited the big picture – your mission, your values, your timeline, et al – it's very tempting to dive right back into action. But movement in and of itself isn't always/necessarily forward motion. Without direction, you may only end up spinning in place, as though on an invisible hamster wheel.

This is where strategic re-entry comes in.

Here's how to bring altitude to alignment:

Step 1: Pause Before You Act (Allow the Clarity to Settle First)

Don't do something on impulse merely because you feel clearer. Breathe. Let the big picture guide – and not simply energize – you.

Ask:

- *"What truly matters now?"*
- *"What's worth doing, and not just doable/possible?"*

Example: As you reflect on your bigger goal of launching your handmade goods shop, you suddenly feel the urge to reorganize your whole workspace. What's needed is to resist the urge and finalize your inventory sheet. That's proper alignment – *choosing clarity over chaos that is disguised as productivity*.

Step 2: Use a Grounding Question to Pinpoint Alignment

Not all subsequent steps and actions are created equal. Some feed your true purpose. Others though, are just mere din disguised as productivity.

Ask:

- *"What is one thing I can do now that my future self will appreciate I chose?"*
- *"If I had to cut everything else out and do just one thing today, what would that be?"*

Step 3: Spot the Difference Between Busy and Aligned

Busy work often just looks like progress. Aligned work, on the other hand, *is actual progress*. Practice distinguishing between the two.

Busy Work Feels Like:

- Inbox zero

- Endless tweaking

- Reactive responses

Aligned Work Feels Like:

- Core priorities

- Forward momentum on important projects

- Activities connected to long-term meaning

For example: Instead of checking every ping from group chats, you sit down and finish prepping for tomorrow's workshop, saving all replies for your next designated time block. It's not as instantly satisfying – *but it's real movement.*

Step 4: Commit to One Next Best Step—and Only One

After you've grabbed onto the aligned action, name it clearly and do it.

Ask:

- *"What's the one thing I can do within the next 15 minutes that benefits the bigger picture?"*

Keep it visible and simple.

With all this covered, it is important to understand that zooming out won't necessarily take away your challenges. However, it will re-size them considerably and help you regain *context*, *direction*, and *control*.

The work will be the very same, but your way of orienting to it will be different.

You now understand how to zoom out and see your actions through a wider lens, so that you can detach from small setbacks and not obsess so much over individual outcomes. And now that you've learned to *see* the bigger picture, you're ready to *learn* from it… especially the failure aspect of it, which far too many of us struggle to digest and process, let alone learn from. The next chapter teaches you how to extract lessons from failure and adjust strategy without needless self-judgment.

CHAPTER 13

REFRAME FAILURE AS FEEDBACK

Failure doesn't mean stop – it means *pay attention*. If you think about it, most of us do not procrastinate before we start… we often procrastinate *after a stumble or two*. Then we start saying to ourselves, "I messed up before." "I couldn't make it work the last time." And that's how the stalling takes over.

But until you put meaning into failure, *it is and remains neutral*. This chapter explores breaking codes of failure – not as a personal flaw, but as useful, often necessary feedback for wiser next steps.

Let's get to it.

I: The Feedback Filter: What Is This Trying to Teach Me?

When something goes wrong, our first reaction, a lot of the time, is usually self-blame:

"*I blew it.*"

"*I'm not good enough for this.*"

"*I always get this wrong.*"

But what if failure isn't a verdict? What if it's just a *signal*? Ever thought of that?

The key difference here is this: Treat every outcome as information and not as a reflection of your worth.

Instead of "Why did I fail?", the better question to ask is:

"*What did this outcome teach me*?'

Here's how to do that in a simple, step-by-step process:

Step 1: Pause the Personal Narrative

Before you examine and interpret the result, you need to first break the reflex habit of blaming yourself.

Write down the outcome as objectively as possible, without judgment.

Example: "*I missed my deadline.*"

Not: "*I'm unreliable.*" Not: "*I blew it again.*" Just: "*The task didn't get done on time.*"

This keeps you in observer mode, which is helpful, and not critic mode, which is very unhelpful.

Step 2: Ask the System Question

Use this reframe:

"What part of my system made this outcome likely?"

Ask yourself:

- Did I underestimate the time this would take?

- Was I working during a low-energy time period?

- Did I expect to feel motivated when I didn't?

- Was I relying on memory rather than a capture system?

Example: *"I didn't prep for the meeting."* → *"I'm relying on reminders in my head rather than booking prep blocks."*

Doing this will allow you to shift from shame to strategy.

Step 3: Spot Misalignments, Not Errors

Failure typically indicates a mismatch:

- Between capacity and expectations

- Between needs and tools

- Between task type and timing

Example: *"I procrastinated on that project"* → not laziness, but a misalignment: *"I didn't understand the first step."*

Misalignment can be fixed... self-blame, on the other hand, is not something you can work with.

Step 4: Document One System Adjustment

Now you ask yourself:

"What will I do differently, based on what I've observed?"

This could be:

- Altering your time-estimation system
- Revising your planning style
- Scheduling a task to an improved energy window

Example: *"Next time, I'll block out 15 minutes the day prior to a meeting for prep. This will be non-negotiable."*

II: Decouple Outcome from Identity

One of the most lethal and silent procrastination habits is this: *confusing what you did with who you are.*

You missed a deadline? An incident, is all this is.

But your brain says: *"I'm not reliable."*

You abandoned a goal once?

Now it's: *"I always quit."*

This sort of identification – tying self to outcome – creates a lot of pressure and shame, not to mention the fear of trying again. It keeps you a *prisoner of the past.*

This sub-chapter teaches you how to spot, stop, and reframe that pattern, so you can move forward without old baggage.

Step 1: Spot Identity Fusion in Your Language

Pay attention to the way you speak following a setback. Identity fusion sounds like this:

- *"I'm just bad at follow-through."*
- *"I never finish things."*
- *"I'm not the type who can stay consistent."*

The issue with statements is they don't characterize the event, which is what should happen; they characterize you, and often permanently.

Step 2: Rephrase Events as Data, Not Traits

Reword your internal monologue in event-based terms:

- *"This project took longer than I expected."*
- *"I hadn't accounted for how tired I'd be."*
- *"I got distracted more today than usual."*

When you do this, you bring facts, *and not judgments*, to the fore.

Example: Replace "*I always mess this up*" with:

> "*This version didn't play out the way I'd wanted. Let me take a look and see why.*"

Step 3: Use the Decoupling Mantra

Add a short interrupting mantra to redirect your internal monologue:

> "*The event isn't me – it's just data.*"

Say it in your head the moment you find yourself going down the spiral. It creates useful mental space. It also reminds you: I am not defined by what happened in the past.

Example: You missed a workout. Instead of thinking "I'm lazy," say:

> "*This skip is just data. The real question is, what derailed me? What can be improved next* time?"

Step 4: Choose an Identity That Allows Mistakes

Rather than striving to protect an intact, perfect self-image, make efforts to step into a growth-oriented one:

- *"I'm someone who learns along the way."*
- *"I'm building reliability, not proving perfection."*

These identities create room for mistakes without defaulting to shame.

Example: Say, you put off writing a report. Instead of "I can't concentrate and perform focused work," say:

> "*I'm learning the skill of focus, and that means it's going to involve stumbles.*"

III: Build a Failure Archive – On Purpose

Most of us tend to bury our failures. We tend to overlook them, or at least try to. But when you never look back, you never actually learn.

Here's a radical idea: don't hide your failures. *Document them. Deliberately.*

Not to beat yourself up, but to build a personal archive of lessons that focuses your future efforts and takes out the sting of getting it wrong.

Done right, this effectively turns "failure" into fuel.

Step 1: Create a Dedicated "Failure Archive" Space

This is your own space to keep track of attempts that didn't go as planned. Call it what you like:

- "Lessons Learned"

- "What Didn't Work"

- "Attempt Log"

Have it in a note-taking app, physical notebook, or document – just one consistent spot that you can access with ease.

Example: You try a morning routine for 7 days and abandon it by Day 3. Instead of forgetting about it, you log it: "Attempted 5AM wake-up with journaling. Was sleep-deprived by Day 3. Journaling became forced. Must change timing and begin more gently."

Step 2: Record the Three Essentials

Every time something fails to live up to expectations, record:

1. What was attempted

(e.g., "*Wrote first blog post*" or "*Scheduled deep work post-lunch.*")

2. What was wrong

(e.g., "*No one read* it" or "*Was too tired to focus.*")

3. What I learned now

(e.g., "*Need distribution plan*" or "*Mornings are best for thinking work.*")

This simple, logical structure enables you *to separate facts from feelings*.

Example Entry:

- Tried: Blocking 4 hours for writing

- Didn't work: Got overwhelmed, procrastinated

- Learned: 4 hours felt overwhelming—working in 30-minute increments might be the way to go

Step 3: Review It Monthly (Briefly, and Not Emotionally)

Once a month, scan the archive. Ask:

- What trends do I see?

- What adjustments have proven fruitful, since?

- What am I no longer avoiding doing again?

Step 4: Rewire Failure as Input, Not Identity

The archive's hidden value, in addition to providing valuable insight, is very necessary for identity recalibration too. It teaches your brain:

- *"I try things."*

- *"I learn things."*

- *"Failure is merely a map, not a stop sign."*

IV: Compare Attempts, Not Just Outcomes

Progress isn't winning. *Progress is willing*. Willing to show up, experiment, and pivot. But most of us only track the end result – "Did it work or not?" – and ignore the most valuable metric: *Did I do it differently*?

This mind-set shift flips *failure to feedback* and *motion into expansion*.

Step 1: Track Starts, Not Just Finishes

Instead of just logging what you finished, begin logging what you attempted as well, especially if it's new, different, or improved from the last version.

Example: I didn't finish editing the entire video, but I tried a new script format.

Create a page in your planner, tracker, or notebook that has dedicated space for:

- *"What I started today"*
- *"What I tried differently"*

Step 2: Measure Iteration, Not Perfection

Track improvements:

- Did you tweak the intro slide to be easier to understand?
- Did you rewrite the email subject line to have more impact?
- Did you adjust your routine to better fit your energy?

Track these micro-changes, as they show that you're improving.

Example: "First job application was rushed. Second one had a tailored cover letter. Third one had a blockbuster summary. Each version = progress – even if no callback yet."

This is how coders, athletes, artists, and builders learn and make successive improvements: test → tweak → retest.

Step 3: Take on the Scientist's Mindset

Start to ask yourself:

- *"What did I test today?"*
- *"What did I modify from yesterday?"*
- *"What is one thing I can modify next?"*

Pivot away from, "*Did it work?*" and towards, "*What did I learn by attempting this?*"

Example: You hosted a webinar that filled poorly. Instead of looking at this as a failure, you ask: "*What day/time got the least clicks? What title did I use?*" Then you adapt and you test again.

Step 4: Let Experiments Define Your Progress Narrative

Frame your progress story around this:

> "*I'm someone who experiments.*"
> "*I don't wait to get it perfect; I collect data and refine.*"
> "*I'm building reps, not just resumes.*"

Example: You look back at your past month and see 8 small experiments logged – task systems, outreach emails, time-boxing strategies. Maybe none of them went viral. But all of them educated you. If you think about it, this is both leverage and momentum wrapped in one.

V: Use Micro-Failure as Part of Practice

Most of us believe that failure is something to be avoided. The truth about true skill-building, however, is that *is based on micro-failure*. It is based on small, low-stakes failures that show that you're very clearly going beyond your comfort or autopilot zone.

When failure is expected (even invited) as part of the learning cycle, it completely loses its emotional sting and, in so doing, *gains practical usefulness*.

Step 1: Normalize Failure as a Training Signal

When you're practicing anything with real intention – writing, coding, speaking, launching, etc. – small failures are inevitable. But they aren't signs you're doing it wrong; they're signs you're engaging with the edges of your ability.

Example: A pro tennis player hits 30 backhands during drills. 10 of them miss completely. The mindset pros like these have is that those misses, as opposed to being shameful or indicators of incompetence, are *data points for adjusting footwork or timing*. And this is what makes the practice work, and their skills and ability to improve, by and by.

Step 2: Design Practice That Includes Breakage

Choose activities just a notch or two above your present ability. Things you can't quite handle yet. Doing this consistently will build up your tolerance for error and turn "failure" into input.

Step 3: De-Tune the Emotional Volume

Don't try to silence micro-failure unease. Instead, turn the volume down on what it implies.

Say the following phrases over and over:

- *"This didn't work, but it taught me something."*
- *"This glitch is a clue, not a verdict."*
- *"This whiff-and-miss is part of building the muscle."*

Step 4: Use Low-Stakes Experiments to Build Desensitization

Pick areas where you can purposefully fail on purpose; small bets that don't cost you too much.

- Post a rough idea online and see what resonates.

- Try a new workflow knowing it might be clunky at first.

- Submit work before you're "ready," with the direct intention to break the over-polishing cycle.

VI: The Growth Reflection: Mine Failure to Refine Strategy

Failure often feels absolute when it's not followed by assessment. But when you don't stop at a failure and critique the process, *and not yourself*, failure becomes a launchpad instead of a dead end.

Growth happens most rapidly not from avoiding mistakes, but from understanding the right lessons after them.

Step 1: Reconnect with the Original Goal

Before analyzing what went wrong, Zoom out: What were you actually attempting to do?

Not what it felt like. Not what other people did. *But what the basic goal was.*

Example: You meant to send a job application. The real goal: *get an entire application in on time*, not "feel confident or polished doing it."

Step 2: Identify What Broke in the *Process*, Not the Person

Don't ask: "*Why did I botch this?*"

Ask: "*Where did the system fail?*"

Look at:

- Timing (Was I in too big a rush?)
- Sequence (Did I skip an essential prep step?)
- Scope (Was the goal too lofty for one session?)
- Tools (Was I using the wrong format or environment?)

Example: Say, you missed a project deadline. Instead of accusing yourself of being lazy, you note down: "*I didn't have a clear midpoint check-in, so I drifted off.*"

"Monitoring mechanics" is what this is.

Step 3: Choose a Micro-Adjustment to Use in the Future

Don't try to fix everything. Just specify one single adjustment you'll make in the future based on what you now know and understand.

Use the formula:

"Next time, I'll [adjustment] so that [desired outcome]."

Example:

"Next time, I'll add a midpoint checkpoint with draft review so I don't lose my way."

Tiny, specific tweaks compound each other to build both better systems and significantly improved results.

To wrap this one up, it is very important that you understand that failure isn't a dead end. In fact, it is quite the opposite; it is a doorway that you can walk through onto greener pastures. You don't grow despite failure; *you grow through it*. The sooner you can examine what went wrong without shame, the sooner you will be able to consistently move forward. Your mistakes are not proof that you can't; they're proof that you're learning… that you're capable of growth. Same applies to any setbacks that stem from your mistakes… take them as directions, not verdicts. And then use them to improve and get better.

You've now learned to reinterpret failure as valuable feedback as opposed to personal defeat. The next natural evolution is to *stop letting feelings govern your progress altogether*. The next chapter, titled **Detach Progress from Mood,** takes this further by showing that action can (and should) continue even without emotional alignment.

Here, you will learn a new mindset shift: that you don't need to *feel like it* to move forward; you just need a reliable system and a healthy relationship with discomfort.

CHAPTER 14

DETACH PROGRESS FROM MOOD

We've all likely been advised at points in our lives to wait until we "feel ready" to begin. But by this point in the book, you should already have some understanding that waiting to feel ready is the enemy of progress. Mood is a very poor compass, all factors considered. Some days are foggy. Some days, torrential. Others calm and clear, etc. But your path doesn't disappear in bad/unideal weather... it stays very much the same. Progress is directional... mood, on the other hand, is just white noise. You don't require perfect conditions to make progress. All you need do, is just continue moving.

This chapter makes for the perfect final chapter of this section since it brings everything together in one ultra-potent, evergreen mental stance: regardless of low motivation, turbulent emotions, lack of clarity, etc.; forward motion is still very much possible.

Let's get to it.

I: Stop Taking Your Emotional Forecast as Instruction

When you wake up tired, irritable, or just feeling off, your mind prefers to take a silent leap: "If I feel this way, then I can't do that today." This is known as emotional forecasting: the false premise that the way you feel right now *is a good indication of how everything will go*.

But moods are not commands. They're not mandates. All they are, are weather forecasts, *not traffic lights*.

Let's get attuned to recognize, translate, and unhook from those projections.

Step 1: Name the Forecast Mentality

Start with noticing when you're treating mood as if it were a rulebook. Common forms include:

- *"I'm too worn out to think clearly"*
- *"I'm not on my game today, I'd better wait"*
- *"If I start now, I'll just mess it up"*

Example: You might tell yourself, "I'm too mentally off today to fix anything properly." Nonetheless, if you push yourself to just start tightening one bolt or organizing your tools, you may find that within 15 minutes, you're fully focused and making steady progress. In this case, the forecast was incorrect.

Step 2: Shift from Forecast to Observation

Instead of obeying the feeling and acting on it, observe it:

- *"I'm noticing I feel slow"*

- *"There's some hesitation and resistance here today"*
- *"I'm sensing some blockage. I shouldn't take this as a reason to quit, but a reminder to take it slow"*

This subtle language shift puts you at arm's length of the emotion/feeling in play. It takes you out of the rain and indoors, where you can gaze out the window at it, assess its severity and perhaps even notice that every passing second, it is steadily subsiding.

Practice: Instead of "*I'm nervous, so I won't be able to get going,*" practice "I'm noticing nervousness, but it may subside once I begin."

This kind of observation reduces the pressure to be "ready" and invites curiosity instead of avoidance.

Step 3: Use the Reframe: Mood Is Information, Not Orders

Embed this mantra:

"*Mood is information, not instruction.*"

What does that mean?

- Mood tells you something about how your current state is, not about your capability
- You can be exhausted and still get going
- You can be off and still generate value
- You can feel scattered and spread thin and still work with structure

Example: On low-energy days, professional athletes can still perform well *because they hold process over feeling*. You can do the same, by *letting behavior lead and letting mood follow*.

Step 4: Act First, Evaluate After

If your emotional weather report says "Not today," *test it*.

Select an infinitesimally small action: open one tab, create one bullet point, send one email, etc. Then rethink and reassess.

Generally, the forecast gets revised once the weather moves.

II: Build Systems That Work Regardless of How You Feel

Emotions change during the course of a day. That's life.

And if your progress is entirely dependent on how alert, motivated, or concentrated you are, you'll for sure lose days to the emotional rollercoaster of feeling.

But systems – small ones included – don't care one bit about your emotions. They push you forward despite them.

The objective here is simple: state-proof your process.

Let's unpack this:

Step 1: Substitute Blank Starts with System Starts

A blank page invites hesitation. A structured prompt lowers the barrier.

System > State Example:

Instead of booting up your laptop to an empty doc, you open a checklist:

- Outline one idea

- Develop idea into three bullet points

- Turn bullets into first paragraph

Even on bad days, a checklist like this will offer frictionless entry and help kickstart momentum.

Step 2: Use Fixed-Time Blocks to Anchor Focus

When energy is depleted, duration-based systems are best.

System > State Example:

Instead of saying, "*I'll work until I'm done*," have:

- 10-minute "activation" sessions

- Pomodoro-sprints (25 minutes on, 5 minutes off)

- Fixed blocks: "*At 2 PM, I do X, no matter how I feel about it*"

Time blocks may not make you feel any more focused than you are, but they are very effective in summoning focus via rhythm. Even when the work feels messy and clunky, *it still moves forward.*

Step 3: Default to Minimum Viable Progress

On off days, don't aim for excellence: *aim for done enough to count.*

Create a personal M.V.P. list: Tasks that, when completed, keep your streak alive.

Examples:

- 1 paragraph, not 1,000 words
- Review one page, not the whole chapter
- Sketch an outline, not a polished draft

System > State Example:

When your brain says, "*We've got nothing,*" your system says, "*Do the bare minimum and clock the win.*" Doing this helps you stay in motion, even if progress is slow.

Step 4: Let the System Do the Work When State Can't

If feelings are weather, *systems are scaffolding.*

When you're stressed, derailed, bored, or exhausted, your system steps in:

- It tells you what to do next
- It gives you permission to do "just this much"
- It builds forward movement out of repetition, not motivation

This is how authentic consistency is built – by having something in place that doesn't need your readiness to start up and stay humming.

III: Separate Mood from Meaning

Our moods don't just affect how we feel.

They also affect *how we view and interpret things around us.*

Low energy/low mood does not just make tasks seem harder and more labored; they also make them seem pointless, disjointed, and almost like a referendum on your ability.

Let's explore how to separate emotional fog *from actual meaning.*

Step 1: Recognize the Mood-Meaning Loop

When you're burned out, demotivated, or drained emotionally; your thinking often catches up with you and throws a wrench into your perspective on both the task at hand, and proceedings tethered to it:

- *"This isn't working."*
- *"I'm not cut out for this."*
- *"This whole thing was a bad idea anyway."*

But what's really happening here?

Well, *Mood → Interpretation Distortion,* is what's happening here.

For instance, say, you're mentally tired after a morning series of meetings. Once back at your workstation, you open your laptop, look at your unfinished task and catch yourself thinking, *"This is stupid – why am I even doing this?"* even when you didn't have such thoughts/concerns about your unfinished task prior to the mental fatigue setting in. This is an example of swings in mood leading to interpretation distortion.

Step 2: Create a Buffer Between Feeling and Meaning

Once you catch those thoughts creeping in, you need to insert a buffer into your psyche that keeps them from latching onto what you know to be true.

Use a simple reframe prompt:

"Am I perceiving this through fatigue, or is it actually so?"

Or say:

"I feel low and unmotivated right now, but that is not to say the task is meaningless."

Notice how you're not dismissing the feeling, but rather *just not letting it rewrite the story*.

Step 3: Normalize Emotional Weather Without Redefining Purpose

Emotional dips are part of any meaningful process. They don't mean your goal is flawed or your path is broken.

For example, if you're working on a project that felt exciting before, but feels dull and empty at present, instead of saying, *"Maybe this isn't worth doing anymore,"* say:

"Right now, it feels dull. But that doesn't mean it really is dull. I'll revisit how it feels once I've rested or made some extra steps toward its completion."

Step 4: Anchor Back to Non-Mood-Based Markers

Sure enough, mood may get to you and sway you *from time to time*. But keep in mind that your original intentions, values, and reasons for starting out *still hold*. Those stay stable and unchanged.

Whenever you find yourself wanting to quit something in the middle of the grind, ask:

- *"Why did I start this in the first place?"*
- *"What did I think about its value before the low mood kicked in?"*
- *"Would I be feeling this way after a good night's sleep?"*

This is how you get to ground meaning *in something steadier than how today feels*.

IV: Use Action to Stabilize Mood — Not the Other Way Around

As we pointed out in this chapter's opening paragraph, we're often conditioned to wait for the "right state ' to get started: Wait until you're in the right mood. Wait until you're in the right frame of mind. Wait until you're ready, etc.

But mood is not fuel for action… in fact, if you think about it, it's more often than not *the aftermath of action*.

So, let's flip this stance:

Step 1: Flip the Default Formula

Rather than…

- "I'll get to working once I feel better"
- "I need to get into the right headspace first"

Try...

- "Doing a little bit might get me into the right headspace.".

Step 2: Anchor to the "Mood Follows Motion" Principle

Adopt a new personal policy:

"Mood follows motion, not the other way around."

Note that this policy doesn't involve shoving your feelings aside/ignoring them. Rather, it involves moving forward with the understanding that *even small steps forward can/likely will regulate how you feel, better than ruminating ever could.*

Why it works:

Action reminds your brain: I'm not stuck. This provides a sense of control and traction, which reduces emotional drag.

Step 3: Use Small Starts as Mood Resets

You don't necessarily need a big win to reset and build momentum. A lot of the time, all you need is *an intentional shift away from paralysis and into motion.*

Utilize a 2- to 5-minute "starter action" if you feel emotionally stuck:

- Open the maintenance checklist and reread the last completed item

- Wipe down your workstation or clean one tool

- Return one client call or send a simple text update

- Rename and sort one receipt or photo in your records

- Do 10 jumping jacks (or pullups/pushups, or whatever) if you're frozen in place and are unable to keep the momentum up

Example: Say you've spent the last 30 minutes hovering around the shop, unsure of where to start on a task. A small action – like tightening a loose handle or labeling one drawer – can get things moving. You may find the resistance fading and your energy stabilizing.

Step 4: Track How Often Motion Lifts Mood

Start keeping track of:

"What did I feel just before I acted? How do I feel now?"

This supports a feedback loop wherein *action is an act of stabilization, not a dependent variable*.

V: Anchor to the Mission, Not the Mood

Mood is akin to weather – capricious, and changes by the hour… sometimes even by the minute.

Mission, on the other hand, is like climate – stable, long-term, and *direction-determining*.

If you steer your day based on your feelings in the moment, you'll almost always end up aimlessly adrift. But if you tie yourself to your underlying "why," regardless of the turbulence perpetuated by your emotions; you automatically create a stabilizing influence that doesn't/won't change, *even if/when everything else does*.

Step 1: Name Your Mood-Proof Mission

What are you committed to, *regardless of your feelings*?

Examples:

- *"I exercise because I care about my health and want to stay fit, not because I have boundless energy levels."*

- *"I lead because people are counting on me, not because I am a perennially confident person."*

- *"I make art because I'm an artist, not because creative ideas come easily to me."*

Step 2: Catch the Mood-to-Mission Substitution

When procrastination kicks in, ask yourself:

"Am I letting today's mood override my greater purpose?"

Mood says:

- *"I don't feel like it."*

- *"This is too hard today."*

- *"I'm not in the right headspace."*

Mission replies:

- *"You don't have to feel like it to begin."*

- *"Hard doesn't mean unworthwhile."*

- *"Your mindset shifts when you move."*

Step 3: Write a "Why" Statement You Can Refer Back to on Low Days

Write down a one-sentence summary of your mission. Keep it on your planner, computer, or workspace.

Prompts:

- *"I do this because ___."*
- *"I show up even when it's hard because ___."*
- *"This work contributes to ___."*

You needn't feel 100% realigned to re-read this. In fact, it works best *when you're not*, and need a fire lit under you so you can keep your forward momentum going.

Step 4: Let Mood Influence the Pace, *Not the Path*

It's okay to proceed slowly on tough days. What is not okay, however, *is to turn back each time thunder claps and the rains fall.*

Allow mood influence your pace, sure enough. But *do not let it influence your path.*

Principle:

Mood dictates how it feels…

Not if it matters.

VI: Create a "Low-Mood Protocol" for Progress

Think of this one as being akin to a *"rainy day" mode for productivity*: not ideal conditions for sure, but functional nonetheless.

Step 1: Write Your Bare-Minimum Task List (When You're in a Good Mood)

Think of this your "emergency kit" – a list of things you can count on doing even when you're tired, down, stressed, or mentally cloudy.

Prompts:

- What are the tasks that I can still get done when I am not at my best?

- What is low-pressure but impactful nonetheless?

- What still matters, even if just a little bit?

Examples:

- Return 2 quick customer calls

- Write one bullet for your end-of-day job report

- Organize 5 receipts or invoices

- Clear off your workbench or front counter

- Read 2 pages of a safety manual or supplier guide

Step 2: Set a 15-Minute Default Work Session

Decision fatigue and overwhelm are often at their worst on low-mood days. As such, you need to predefine a brief work session you can start *without negotiation.*

Use a timer. Pick a task. Sit with it for just 15 minutes.

That's it.

This is your non-negotiable "motion ritual." Even if you stop completely after 15 minutes, you've nonetheless shown that action is still possible, even on bad days.

Step 3: Appoint a Check-In Anchor

This can be:

- A trusted friend

- An accountability partner/ "task buddy"

- A daily journal question that only takes a minute or two

- A 2-minute voice note that you record for your own ears

Why is this important? Well, for *human grounding* purposes.

Sometimes, the fastest and surest spur back to forward motion *is the awareness that someone – or something – is holding the line with you.*

Step 4: Print or Save This Protocol Where You Can See It

When you're having a low day, you won't want to set up a system right in the thick of the emotions and turbulence you're grappling with – *you'll want to be reminded of it,* so it can help you hop back onto the progress train.

Put this protocol somewhere frictionless and easy to access: your planner, your phone's notes app, a sticky note on your desk, etc.

Label it:

"*Use This When I Feel Like Doing Nothing.*"

Once you train yourself to think of discipline as "freedom from emotional whiplash", you'll have a much easier time with procrastination. When you're able to act without waiting for your mood to give you permission, it becomes very possible to reclaim consistency. Your emotions will always be there, *and that's fine*. But let them ride along, not actively drive you. Your mood can sit on the passenger side… just don't hand it the keys.

With Reset and Rewiring covered comprehensively, up next, is Section III, which explores Moving Forward and Staying There.

SECTION 3

MOVE FORWARD AND STAY THERE

Now that you've escaped the loop, the next step is to make absolutely sure that you *don't go back*. As such, this final section is all about *sustainable momentum*. You'll learn how to build strong habits without burning out, chunk big goals into bite-sized wins, stay productive consistently, etc. The goal of this section is to help you become someone who follows through and "stays following through" *even when life is (a lot) less than perfect*.

Let's get to it.

CHAPTER 15

BUILD GOOD HABITS THAT STICK

Habits are the foundation that keeps you steady when willpower is low... *permanent frameworks, as opposed to molds*. As such, the real question, with regard to habits, isn't "How do I start?" It's: *"What makes a habit stick once the honeymoon period ends?"*

We have positioned this chapter in a *forward-facing, future-resilient* way. Instead of covering habit *creation* in general or as emotional support (which we've already done implicitly up to this point), we'll anchor this chapter in *building upward compounding structures* that reinforce your identity, allow for flexibility, and withstand life's disruptions.

Let's get to it.

I: Attach Habits to Identity, Not Outcomes

Most of us work to build habits by chasing after results.

For instance, we may say to ourselves: "*I will go to the gym to lose some weight.*"

Or: "*I will study to earn an A on the test.*"

But the problem with result-oriented habits is this:

When results lag, motivation tends to run out fast.

You need habits that do not depend on results to keep going. You also need habits that protect identity; *habits that feel like proof of who you are.*

Let's set up that foundation:

Step 1: Notice Where You're Chasing, Not Becoming

Start with these questions:

- Why am I doing this habit?
- Am I doing it to prove something short-term, or to express something long-term?

Examples:

- "*I meditate to lessen anxiety*" → chase-based
- "*I meditate because I'm a person who appreciates inner calm*" → identity-based

Chase-based habits *are conditional.* Identity-based habits, on the other hand, *are anchored.* They're less breakable, much more organic, and a lot easier to redirect back to.

Step 2: Flip the Habit into a Who-Statement

Every habit *is a silent vote on what you believe yourself to be*. Keep this in mind as you build/assess your habits.

So instead of "*I want to make more art*," say:

> "*I'm an artist, and artists make art, even/especially when it's dry, clunky, or unpolished.*"

It is paramount that you *turn your habit into an identity echo*.

Here are a couple of examples:

- *"I'm learning French"* → *"I'm someone who enjoys stretching past my mother tongue."*
- *"I'm reading to become smarter"* → *"I'm a thinker. I sharpen through ideas."*
- *"I'm attempting to wake up early"* → *"I'm a person who respects and cherishes my early mornings."*

Hook the action to who you are – or who you're developing into.

Step 3: Use the Identity Question as a Cue

Build a habit check-in for this question:

> "*What would a person like me do next?*"

- "*I'm a person who gets things done*" → So I'll follow through on this task, brief as it is, before switching apps.
- "*I'm a person who pays attention to my health*" → So I stretch before bedtime.

- *"I'm a builder who builds steadily and without much fuss"* → So I'll show up today without waiting to be/feel ready/motivated.

This cue gently *replaces overthinking with internal alignment.*

Step 4: Make Identity Your Return Point, Not Your Reward

When habits fail, most folks abandon them because the result hasn't come yet.

Identity-based habits, on the other hand, are habits that are self-reinforcing. You return to them because they feel like home... and home is where the heart is.

So even if your weight doesn't budge one bit, you say:

> *"I still exercise, because I'm someone who respects their body."*

Even if the followers don't grow, you say:

> *"I still post, because I'm someone who values the world and has valuable input that I need to get out there."*

II: Design Your Environment to Reinforce the Habit Automatically

Willpower is overrated. Overestimated. Environment, on the other hand, is massively underappreciated.

In order to create an automatic state of habit, you can't rely on motivation or mood, fleeting as they are. What you need to do, is to actively design your environment *so that it provides the path of least resistance* to your goals.

Your job isn't to assert discipline onto yourself… it's to weed out resistance.

Step 1: Create Passive Cues in Your Physical Environment

Your brain responds to what it perceives, *not necessarily to what it ought to pay attention to/knows is important.*

Take advantage of this:

- Put pen and journal on pillow → Writing becomes a bedtime activity.

- Put exercise shoes by door → Movement/exercise automatically becomes something you feel compelled to do.

- Put guitar on stand, not in case → Practice is now only one quick motion away.

Basically, make the habit of leaving your habit tools *always ready and accessible*, so they feel like the natural next move every single time.

Step 2: Remove Hidden Sabotage Elements in Your Digital Environment

Digital surroundings can hijack your habits unbeknownst to you.

Re-engineer your digital defaults:

- Toggle your phone screen to grayscale → Significantly reduces dopamine-driven app use.

- Set your notes app or writing document on your desktop → First click = habit start.

- Use a distraction blocker (e.g., block social media during creative blocks) → Instills deliberate work habits.

Example: If your goal is to read more, set your browser's home page to your online reading list, *not a news site, sports page or YouTube*.

Step 3: Create a "Friction Map" of Your Environment

Ask:

What in my environment makes the right habit difficult, and the wrong habit convenient?

Then flip it.

- Tuck snacks away in a cabinet rather than on the counter.
- Charge your phone across the room, not on your bed or workstation.
- Place your yoga mat right where you can step over it, when you get up in the morning.

When it takes effort to do the wrong thing, and doing the right thing becomes the default, *your own behavior ultimately follows suit without a fight*.

Step 4: Align Your Social Environment with the Habit

Other people are very much part of your environment as well.

Ask yourself:

- Who helps normalize the new habit I am trying to integrate?
- Who makes the old behavior feel normal or validated?

You don't have to get rid of them, but you can certainly set boundaries to offset the perpetuation of older habits that they may (unwittingly) facilitate:

- Explain what you are trying to do, to someone who already does/practices the things/ideals you're aiming for.

- Join a community where your target habit is the norm.

- Spend less time in places where your effort is mocked, not mirrored.

Put yourself in positions where social proximity enforces personal consistency.

III: Create Routines That Are Modular, Not Rigid

What's the most destructive thought when trying to build a habit? Well, this one:

"If I can't do it perfectly, I won't do it at all."

This is the all-or-nothing trap, and it is the number one silent assassin of consistency.

Rigid routines shatter under pressure. Flexible routines, on the other hand, bend and live on.

The solution is simple: Don't create your habit as one fixed size… create it to scale.

Step 1: Design a Flexible Habit in Tiers

Frame your habit with modular layers – different levels of intensity for different days.

Example: A journaling habit

- Tier 1 – 2-minute quick dump: Single sentence or bullet.

- Tier 2 – 10-minute reflection: Single page or prompt response.

- Tier 3 – Deep dive: Full journaling session, 20+ minutes.

Step 2: Match the Module to the Day's Energy

Instead of "*Can I do the habit today?*", ask:

"*Which version of the habit matches today's energy?*"

Examples:

- Exercise habit → 5 push-ups / 15-minute walk / full workout

- Study habit → Flashcard review / focused Pomodoro / full chapter

- Creative habit → Title ideas / 1 draft paragraph / 1-hour session

Reframing habits like this effectively takes guilt out of the equation so that you're not failing anymore, but constantly adapting.

Step 3: Design a Pre-Written Menu of Your Habit Modules

Pre-plan your routine so it is scale-friendly.

Create a menu like:

- Low energy version

- State-of-the-art version
- Check-high focus version

Write it down and save it in an easily accessible place so you can refer to it easily.

With a menu like this, you don't have to rack your brains and hesitate on bad days anymore… *you simply pick the mode and get rolling.*

Reminder phrase for you: "*Always something*" beats "*sometimes perfect.*"

Step 4: Monitor Wins, Not Versions

Don't just reward the max version… make the habit of viewing every completed module *as a habit successfully maintained, and thus one worthy of praise.*

If you:

- Walked for 3 minutes instead of skipping
- Doodled instead of painting
- Composed a messy paragraph instead of holding out for inspiration

…you stayed in motion.

You honored the habit, and in so doing kept its identity alive.

IV: Make the Cue Obvious and the Start Automatic

Good habits don't just stick because they're significant/meaningful… they stick because they start themselves.

Initiation, not discipline, is the real key to longevity.

When we don't know when or how a habit starts, we tend to fall back on delay. But if a trigger is stark and obvious, and built into our environment or routines, the habit kickstarts almost without thought.

Your job here, *is to make that start frictionless*:

Step 1: Create a Clear, Visible Trigger

Every habit needs a trigger… something that invites it into action.

Make your cue/trigger tangible… something you can touch, and something that's specific.

Examples:

- Place your journal and pen on your pillow
  → evokes evening journaling

- Leave your running shoes in the entryway
  → evokes morning motion/exercise

- Place a water bottle beside your workspace
  → evokes steady/adequate water consumption

Step 2: Link It to a Current Anchor

The habits that will work best for you are the ones *that piggyback on habits you already have*.

This is known as habit stacking – *pinning a new action/desired habit onto an old anchor*.

Examples:

- After brushing teeth → stretch for 60 seconds
- After making coffee → open to-do list
- After booting up computer → read goals for 2 minutes

The old behavior serves as the launchpad for the new one.

Step 3: Remove Ambiguity from the Start

Imprecise habits die young.

> "I'll exercise today"
> ...turns into "Maybe later."

But:

> "When I've finished breakfast, I'll walk for 10 minutes."
> ...starts itself.

Make the cue clear; make the trigger moment clear, and remove any/all guesswork completely. A habit that begins with clarity is one that you're far more likely to follow through for the long haul.

Step 4: Design the Start in a Way that Makes It Impossible to Skip

You don't need to automate the whole habit here – just the first 30 seconds.

Make the first move obvious and brainless.

Examples:

- Habit: Meditation
  Start: Your alarm on your phone rings → sit down in your chair immediately

- Habit: Journaling
  Start: You open your laptop and the first tab is your journaling app

- Habit: Reading
  Start: Your book is already on your pillow when you go to bed

Once you get moving, momentum takes over.

V: Track Progress Without Turning It into Pressure

Tracking can be powerful. It can also be extremely incapacitating as well.

Utilized well, it builds self-knowledge, facilitates routine, and gives form and structure to intangible progress. Utilize it poorly, on the other hand, and it becomes a leaderboard of shame.

This section teaches a simple, albeit fundamental principle: *Track for visibility, not judgment*.

The purpose here is to notice, not grade:

Step 1: Choose a Light Approach to Tracking

Start with tools that show up without weighing you down. These tools are not meant to measure performance, but to help you see yourself showing up.

Examples:

- Habit Chain Calendar: Make an X every time you do the habit. The goal of this, is to keep the chain going.

- 3-Word Daily Summary: At the close of each day, write three words that summarize your effort or mindset (e.g., "*showed up tired*" or "*quick but solid*").

- Weekly Micro-Review: At the end of each week, reflect and ask yourself:

  "*What worked*?"
  "*What felt hard*?"
  "*What's next*?"

Step 2: Focus on Continuity, Not Quantity

Most habits fall apart when we focus on how much we're doing, *as opposed to whether we're staying committed to the journey and maintaining.*

For example, don't measure how long you meditated or how many pages you wrote.

Just mark: Did I work on the habit today?

Why this works: You reinforce identity expression (i.e., "*I'm a meditator*") instead of chasing ever-bigger numbers that ultimately become unachievable.

Step 3: Watch for the Pressure Creep

Even light tracking can become pressure if you let it.

Signs you've tipped over:

- You miss the habit because it "*won't be a good session today*"

- You feel *shame* about missing a day, *not curiosity*

- You characterize a small win as a "not enough" narrative

If this is happening, step back. Then, calmly remind yourself:

"This is a signal. This is not the endpoint and neither is it a score."

Tracking is supposed to keep you connected, *not to win points*.

Step 4: Make Review a Ritual

Set aside a regular time to glance at your tracker *in a spirit of curiosity, and not criticism.*

Ask:

- *"What patterns do I see?"*

- *"Where did the habit feel easy? Where did it resist?"*

- *"What tweak could support next week's version of me?"*

This helps to make habit-forming a growing process, and not a test that you're trying to either continually pass or fail.

VI: Build Failure Tolerance into the Habit

The habits that endure aren't necessarily the ones that you never slip up on… a lot of the time, they're the ones you repeatedly snap back to after failure – swiftly, calmly, and with no fanfare.

If you think about it, most of us don't quit because we skip a day. We quit because skipping a day *causes shame, which causes avoidance, which results in abandonment.* Make sense?

To make a habit enduring, *it needs to accept imperfection as a fundamental design requirement.*

Step 1: Normalize Misses in Advance

Missing a habit isn't a failure; it's a statistical inevitability. Illness, travel, fatigue, distraction… it happens.

So, design your habit *with real life* in mind.

Adopt the rule:

> *"One skip is normal. Two skips, on the other hand, is a decision."*

Step 2: Insert a Swift Reset Trigger

Create one, automatic reminder that says *"it's time to bounce back after a skip."*

Could be:

- A weekly Sunday night calendar check-in.

- A brief question: "*What habit did I skip this week, and how do I shrink it to restart?*"

- A sticky note on your desk: "*Today is always a good day to get back on track once more.*"

This helps to break the "I'll get back to it later" spiral.

Step 4: Redefine a Successful Habit

Not as: "*I do this every day, no matter what.*"

But as:

> "*This is something I come back to easily… even when I drift off.*"

If your habit only works if life/everything is perfect, then it's most certainly not built for real life.

This chapter has taught you how to *build sustainable habits*. Now that you're sufficiently set up with momentum-friendly habits and routines, the next concern is sustainability. As such, the logical follow-up is *avoiding burnout while still making progress*.

The next chapter explores this in detail.

CHAPTER 16

GET THINGS DONE WITHOUT BURNING OUT

A lot of the time, burnout doesn't occur because you worked too hard – it comes about because you *worked without replenishment,* and ran yourself into the ground as a result. No recovery, no sense of purpose, no control... you name it. Just constant, incessant output with no closure. And once burnout sets in, procrastination is usually nipping at its heels.

This chapter won't teach you how to avoid burnout by doing less... doing so would only perpetuate procrastination, really. What this chapter will do, is show you exactly how to work *in a way that doesn't burn you out.*

Let's get to it.

I: Use a Weekly Altitude Review (And Not a Daily Hustle Loop)

One of the most underrated causes of procrastination is *trying to win every day*.

When every day is a pressure cooker of *obligations*, *perfectionism*, and *deadlines*, your brain often just defaults to avoidance. This causes you to delay and procrastinate, and you ultimately burn out trying to keep up a pace that's quite frankly impossible.

Step 1: Shift from Daily Stress to Weekly Pacing

Instead of waking up with a "How do I dominate today?" mentality, *zoom out* and ask yourself, "Where exactly does this week call for a *push* – and where does it call for a *pause*?"

Doing this will help reframe your effort into a smooth, steady 7-day cadence, as opposed to successive (and very draining) 24-hour sprints.

Why it matters:

When you set yourself up to accomplish too much, every task begins to feel heavy. That heaviness creates hesitation, which, when stacked up, leads to overwhelm. Overwhelm ultimately yields inertia.

But when you focus on the big picture, momentum becomes manageable. You no longer fuss and worry over "falling behind" after one unideal, low-energy day, *because the rest of the week cushions it*.

Step 2: Design a Weekly Flow That Prevents Avoidance Loops

Create a rhythm your brain can't resist.

- One "Heavy Day": Set aside a day for your heaviest work (intensive focus, important deadlines, high-intensity sessions).

- One "Light Day": Schedule in recovery time, admin, or affect-neutral work.

- Two to Three "Flex Days": Provide space for flexibility. Life is unpredictable, moods change… and so should your schedule.

Example:

You reserve Wednesday for hands-on repairs, Monday for supply runs and admin, and Thursday for client meetings or spill-over tasks. That structure eliminates decision fatigue—and with it, the tendency to push things off for "later."

The more distinctive the flow, the fewer-and-further-between the stalls.

Step 3: Conduct a Sunday (or Start-of-Week) "Altitude Review"

Schedule 15 minutes to "plan above the weeds":

- What 1-3 key results would make this week's progress truly significant?

- What are the days which feel naturally heavier or lighter in energy or demands?

- Where do I carve out space for unexpected interruptions – so I don't fall apart the moment things get bad?

Step 4: Evaluate Progress by the Week (Not by the Day)

At the end of the week, swap guilt-based thoughts like:

"I didn't do enough today."

with:

"Did I advance the right things and elements this week?"

This keeps you protected from the "one bad day = failure" thinking that all too often triggers procrastination spirals. Even when Tuesday unravels horribly, your Wednesday and Thursday are still poised to advance the week. This kind of attitude keeps you constantly progressing, and not stuck in shame.

Why This Kills Procrastination

When you no longer require high performance on a daily basis, you reduce the pressure that often leads to avoidance. When you spread your effort over a week, your brain sees space instead of threat. And when your brain is conditioned to anticipate life's rhythm this way, it no longer catches you off-guard/unprepared. This helps you procrastinate less *because you factored in imperfection.*

II: Assign Emotional Weight to Your Tasks — Not Just Time

Procrastination generally has less to do with how long it takes…

…and *everything to do with how heavy it feels*.

Most task lists treat time as if it is the only variable that matters:

"30 minutes for email" "1 hour for writing" "5 minutes for invoicing."

Here's the catch, though:

Some 5-minute tasks feel considerably heavier emotionally than some 2-hour projects.

And that friction – which the vast majority of us fail to even consider, let alone factor in – is a very potent driver of procrastination.

Step 1: Understand the Psychological Burden Behind Tasks

From today, henceforth, start asking: How does this task feel... not just how long will it take?

Most of the things we procrastinate about aren't necessarily big in time. They're just big in resistance:

- A 3-minute follow-up call? → fear of confrontation = draining

- A 5-minute tool check? → mental friction = draining

- A 1-hour furniture build? → if it's flow-inducing = energizing

See what we're talking about here? Your brain usually isn't resisting the time taken to perform the task – the emotional discomfort is what it resists.

Step 2: Flag Your High-Friction Tasks in Advance

As you go over your to-do's, label them like this:

- High-friction / High-resistance

Tasks that invoke dread, avoidance, or emotional work
(e.g., addressing an unpleasant person, correcting mistakes, uncertain responses)

- Neutral or Admin Load

Plain but repetitive or mildly boring

(e.g., making appointments, planning content)

- Low-friction / Flow-Based

Tasks that are natural or stimulating

(e.g., generating ideas, deep writing, crafting something)

With a layout like this, you're effectively working with reality, *not fantasy*, and you won't be as likely to cram six draining things into one day and then wonder why you just "can't buckle down and stay focused."

Step 3: Use the 1:2 Burnout Prevention Ratio

Here's a sustainable rhythm to help avoid procrastination before it takes root:

For every *draining* activity, schedule at least *two neutral or lightweight* ones.

This effectively injects psychological balance into your day. Instead of creating friction repeatedly, you stack your energy and effort in a manner that your brain doesn't resist.

Example:

- Respond to that nagging client email
- Then spruce up your virtual desktop
- Then tidy up yesterday's flow-based draft

You'll still get the hard stuff done, but *you won't be bogged down because of cumulative weight*.

Step 4: Create a "Light Stack" List for Recovery Days

Procrastination, as we've explained, tends to spike on off-days – when experiencing low energy/mood dips, or after emotionally draining activities.

That's where your *Light Stack list* comes in:

This is your predetermined list of flow-based or neutral activities you can fall back on without negotiation:

- Sort bookmarks
- Read saved research
- Reformat slides
- Tidy up workspace

This keeps momentum engaged without forcing false/pretend productivity or crashing and burning.

III: Build Capacity Days and Catch-Up Buffers

Contrary to what you may think/how it appears on the surface; when *every single hour* is spoken for, *procrastination often becomes inevitable*.

This is because the *system you're running can't breathe*. There's just no space for it.

As we mentioned, most productivity plans assume everything will go right: Deadlines will be hit, moods will be steady, tasks will stay in scope, etc. But as we've already established, that's just not real life.

Real life is late beginnings… it's surprise delays, low-energy mornings, one-task overruns, et al.

As such, when your calendar has no margin, one slip is usually likely to turn into a full-blown avoidance spiral that drives your entire day into a reef.

Step 1: Understand Why "Fully Booked" = Fragile

Too many of us think that packed schedules are a badge of discipline.

But here is what's really happening:

- No room to catch up = burnout trap

- No room for spillovers = fragile structure

- No buffer time = each glitch puts the entire framework at the risk of collapse

When you're fully booked, you don't stave off procrastination… you actually just raise its probability, because you've left no room for slow starts, do-overs, or redirecting, which often leads to your brain steering clear of starting altogether.

Step 2: Introduce "Capacity Space" in Your Week

Capacity space is pre-built, commitment-free time, dedicated to performing one of three critical tasks:

1. Overrun Catch-Up

→ For when work takes more time than estimated (it always does by the way)

2. Mental Reset

→ For decompression or low-priority work that restores energy

3. Flexible Focus Time

→ For unexpected priorities or creative meandering

Think of this as structural space meant to cushion reality, and undercut resistance to starting.

Example:

Set aside two 90-minute chunks per week that are unscheduled, but protected.

No deadlines. No appointments. Just open space for recovery or rerouting.

Step 3: Use "Catch-Up Buffers" to Fight Avoidance Loops

Let's say Monday slipped away and Tuesday was ultra-packed.

If you don't have buffers, your brain starts to think: "Well, that's two days down. There's really no point catching up now."

And that's how the procrastination slide often begins.

But if you've already made space for Thursday to be light, you won't freak out like you would have, otherwise; *you shift*. You jam those missed essentials into your buffer block, and steer your week back on track.

Step 4: Redefine Efficiency as Resilience, *Not Density*

True productivity, rather than being about filling every slot available, is about *how efficiently your system can handle pressure/friction.* Very few people actually understand this, which is why so many of us have issues with maintaining consistent productivity.

A plan that breaks under pressure isn't efficient.

It's brittle. Stiff. Likely to crash.

So, don't mistake "busy" with "disciplined."

Start designing for slack, recovery, and adjustment room.

Those are the friction-busters that effectively kill procrastination at the root, seeing as how *you're no longer in fear of the fallout of imperfect momentum.*

IV: Ration Your Yeses (Burnout Often Begins with Overcommitment)

Many a time, procrastination begins with a full schedule, built on too many 'yeses.'

You said yes to the favor.

Yes, to the extra meeting.

Yes, to helping out – when you were already at full capacity.

So, the pressure builds, deadlines accrue, and before you know it, your brain revolts: "I can't do any of this now."

The real issue here, is that you traded your freedom, *one yes at a time.*

Step 1: Rephrase the Problem – Not "Too Much to Do," But "Too Much Agreed To"

Burnout is not typically the result of sheer quantity… it's the result of *unfiltered access.*

Every unchecked ask is yet another transaction involving time, energy, and attention – resources already thin.

Procrastination, thus, shows up and takes root not because you can't, *but because you're over-committed*, with each assignment feeling like an obligation instead of a choice. This discourages motivation and nurtures procrastination.

Step 2: Use "Let Me Get Back to You" as a Default Pause

Practice *inserting a buffer pause* between question and answer:

> "*Let me check my availability and get back to you.*"
> "*I'd be happy to consider it – can I call you tomorrow?*"

This gives you time to assess whether the ask truly aligns with your current priorities. It also stops the knee-jerk habit of reactive "yes-ing" that ultimately leads you into procrastination loops and traps.

Step 3: Turn to Output Quotas, Not "People Quotas"

Instead of tracking the number of people you've helped, *start tracking how much high-quality output you've generated.*

Ask:

- *"What kind/quality/quantity of work do I need to ship this week?"*
- *"How many deep-focus sessions do I need to protect?"*

That's your sweet spot, and you need to protect it with all the seriousness you can muster.

When a new request threatens that output, it stops being a scheduling choice (if it ever was one in the first place) and becomes a full-blown productivity tax.

Example:

You must finish a service quote by Friday. A teammate asks for "just one quick look at a separate project."

It may seem trivial – and maybe it is overall – but right now, it costs you *attention*, *recovery time*, and *forward motion*.

If it doesn't meet your output needs, then it doesn't fit your week, and the thing to do is to politely decline and perhaps ask for an optimal re-schedule.

Step 4: Build a 3-Tier Request Filter

Protect your attention with a *basic, easy-to-digest* decision matrix for new requests:

1. Instant Yes → Aligns directly with your goal and bandwidth

2. Delayed Decision → Worth considering, but needs thinking through

3. Default No → Non-aligned, unnecessary, or people-pleasing driven

Do expect most requests to fall into tier 2 or 3.

Treat tier 1 as holy ground – be very, very painstaking about what you say yes to.

And don't forget:

"No" is not rejection. It's respect – *for your time, your attention, and your long-game energy.*

V: Define Your "Enough" Threshold and Protect It

One of the sneakier procrastination accelerants is this particular line of thinking:

"No matter what I do… it's not enough."

This is a trap for your mind that not only results in burnout; it undermines direction too.

Without a defined finish line, everything becomes infinite. And when everything is infinite, your mind feels like it has no choice but to autopilot into delay. Because… why bother starting something if completion and fulfilment are unviable?

To stay safe from burnout and stultification stemming from perfectionism, you need a daily boundary – a line beyond which you can genuinely say:

"I've done enough. I can stop without guilt."

Step 1: Decide What "Enough for Today" Is – Before the Day Begins

Before your day gets underway, *determine what constitutes a win.*

Ask:

- *"If I only got these three done, would I feel grounded and at ease?"*

- *"What version of today would make me feel able to sleep soundly tonight without after-ruminations?"*

This gives your mind something it can focus on and wrap up.

What is more, when you have permission to stop, you are actually more likely to opt in and keep plugging away.

Example: Instead of striving for a spotless workspace, you decide:

"Today, if I clear the top 10 items off this counter, that's good enough."

Doing this helps you move out of endless tinkering and into focused execution—which shuts down the procrastination window.

Step 2: Set a "Minimum Meaningful Progress" Marker for the Week

Weekly progress shouldn't be tethered to quantity – it needs to be about intentional progress forward.

Try asking yourself:

- *"What's one deliverable or improvement that would make this week be worth it?"*

- *"If everything else falls apart, what would I feel accomplished to have at least tried at?"*

You've now set a baseline that's achievable and fulfilling to aim for and accomplish.

Anything beyond that is bonus. It shouldn't be a source of stress.

Example:

If you're a programmer learning to code, your weekly "enough" could be:

"Complete one small project and reflect on what I learned."

No pressure to master everything… just consistent progress.

Step 3: Define the Endpoint – Then Stop Tweaking

Without a deliberate endpoint, lots of people find themselves bogged down in compulsive polishing or fear-based delay.

You can't finish what you won't allow to get finished.

So, ask beforehand:

- *"What specifically will signal that this project is complete?"*
- *"What scope am I shooting for?"*
- *"What version qualifies as good enough to move on/build from/on, respectively?"*

Once those are set, *honor them to the fullest.* Otherwise, you'll keep the tab open forever.

Step 4: Use "Close the Tab" Rituals to Mark Psychological Completion

Even after you've got the work done, your brain may still not get the memo.

As such, it is necessary to create easy rituals to tell your system when/that it's okay to let go.

Examples:

- Saved file as "FINAL" or moved it to a shipped directory

- Writing a one-line summary of what you got done

- Specifically closing the tab or turning off a workspace light

- Saying out loud, "That's done for today. Time to reboot."

These micro-signals are important, as they help get your brain into closure, and out of task tension. And that closure helps create space for *recovery*, *reflection*, and *relaxation*.

Now that we've established how to work in a way that protects energy, you're now ready to *maximize focus*. Burnout often comes from scattered attention. As such, the next chapter will directly build onto this one by zooming into sharpening focus and eliminating friction.

CHAPTER 17

TRAIN YOUR FOCUS, KILL DISTRACTIONS

Too many people believe that the ability to focus is a gift, and that that's the reason why some have fewer issues mustering it up than others. This is misguided though. Focus isn't a gift at all – it's a skill. It's something that you can work on and improve upon consistently. You don't need to be naturally disciplined to maintain high focus for considerable periods of time; you just need to train your attention like a muscle. This chapter will focus on building your *focus stamina* and *identifying the distraction triggers* that may be presently blunting your edge and causing you to procrastinate.

Let's get to it.

I: Create a "Focus Launch Pad" Ritual

Procrastination, generally, has a lot to do with *mental inertia…* that amorphous, shapeless moment *between intention and initiation*. It can stretch on for hours – if not days – when you don't know how to begin.

This is where the *Focus Launch Pad* comes in. A Focus Launch Pad is a short, repeatable transition ritual that preps your attention and signals, "*We're entering the work zone now.*"

Step 1: Choose a Sensory Anchor That Signals "Start

Sensory cues speed up state transitions. Choose one cue that you associate with focus:

- Sound: Play a specific instrumental song on repeat.

- Smell: Light a candle or use a drop of essential oil.

- Visual: Turn your screen to a full-screen workspace or blank page.

Uniformity, not variation, is the goal here. One cue, every time. This will condition your brain so that it eventually internalizes: this sound/smell/screen = deep work.

Step 2: Do a 1-Minute Reset to Clear "Carryover Clutter"

Procrastination feeds on leftover noise from whatever came before it – tabs, messages, thoughts, etc.

Take 60 seconds to:

- Close all non-task-related tabs/apps

- Jot down any non-task-related thoughts in a "Later" list

- Take one deep breath or do one stretch

Think of this as clearing the desk before laying out the task.

Step 3: Set a Visible, Specific Task Target

Ambiguity invites avoidance. Begin by writing on your Launch Pad:

"In this block, I will do: _____ "

Get specific and keep it brief and to the point... not "Finish report," but "Write intro paragraph, etc."

This will help transform the vague "get started" feeling into an actual mission.

Step 4: Perform the Ritual Exactly the Same Way Every Time

Run your Launch Pad the same way every day – even if it's just:

- Light candle → close apps → breathe → start timer

Predictability limits resistance. The more routine the ritual, the less room for doubt or hesitation there is.

II: Train Your Recovery Speed – Not Just Your Focus Span

Focus isn't just the ability to focus. It also encompasses the ability to re-focus; to get back on track and keep moving after losing track.

Most of us often confuse a slip for a stop... a singular distraction leads to shame, which leads to avoidance, etc.... and before you know it, you are hours/days off-track.

World-class focus, however, isn't a perfect streak. It is, more than anything really, *a practiced recovery*.

Let's shorten that rebound time.

Step 1: Neutralize the Slip Moment (No Shame, Just Signal)

If you catch yourself drifting, do everything you can to refrain from self-blame. Self-blame only strengthens the avoidance loop.

Rather, neutrally label it:

- *"I just derailed."*
- *"That's a break in focus. Time to rejoin."*

Even a simple "reset" said aloud can create a pattern-interrupt. The trick here, is in removing moral weight completely from the equation.

Step 2: Return with a Pre-Chosen "Restart Cue"

Have a default behavior that ignites your return to task without fail.

Examples:

- Walk back to the item you were last organizing
- Re-open your checklist or job card
- Set a 3-minute timer and review the last task you completed

Ideally, this ought to be a small prompt that is automatic in nature. You don't mull over it… you just start the motion so that momentum picks up from there.

Step 3: Run a 3-Minute Micro-Reboot (Not a Full Session)

Don't attempt to "get back into the zone" right away. This will likely only lead to overwhelm, which will lead to even more stalling.

Instead:

- Reserve 3 minutes of still task re-immersion

- Don't expect or evaluate flow – just move hands, eyes, or words on the page

- Clarity and rhythm will return once motion gathers speed

Procrastination is usually *less about the break/gap in productivity, and more about not knowing how to get back.*

Step 4: Monitor Recoveries, Not Streaks

Mark times when you came back.

It may be a casual tally or brief notebook entry: "*Lost my focus at 2:10, regained by 2:15.*"

Honoring recovery trains and conditions your identity: "*I get back fast*" > "*I never fall apart.*"

III: Use "Temptation Bundling" to Eliminate Internal Resistance

You don't need to kill every urge.

You just need to *stop obeying them the instant they show up.*

If you think about it, procrastination is heavily tethered to emotional resistance. You want to buckle down and get started on the task, but your mind is like, "*Let's just take a look at this YouTube short real quick. It's literally only ten seconds long anyway.*"

That ten second YouTube short then spirals into fifteen similar shorts, and the task you were trying to do becomes yet another thing to feel guilty about.

To help with this, you need smarter incentives.

Enter *Temptation Bundling*:

Step 1: Understand the Psychology of Temptation Bundling

Temptation bundling pairs something you want to do *with something you have to do*.

You're not denying your urges – you're simply putting them on a leash.

Think about it like this:

"I get X after I do Y."

Why it works:

- It builds anticipation instead of resistance

- It rewards follow-through, not avoidance

- It conditions your mind to associate focus with pleasure – and not just with effort

This is the reverse of productivity based on guilt… dopamine-friendly discipline, so to speak.

Step 2: Create Micro-Bundles That Reinforce Focus

Pick a small, enjoyable reward… then tie it to a completed focus session.

Here are some examples that work well for procrastination:

Focus Work	Reward
45-minute deep work session	Listen to your favorite playlist or podcast
Finish a grueling/uncomfortable task	Take a guilt-free 10-min walk or scroll
Submit something that's been stuck	Watch an episode, snack, or check social
Morning planning session done	Sip your coffee while reading something fun

Important: Do NOT blend the two. The reward comes *after*. It does not come *during*. Blurred boundaries will only turn this into just another distraction loophole. This brings us to the next step…

Step 3: Create a Default "Earn It First" Rule

One effective way to curb procrastination is to ritualize your reward reasoning.

Instead of struggling with each whim to check, scroll, or click – install a clear policy:

"Nothing indulgent until I complete [my first focus block / one critical task / 30 minutes of work]."

Examples:

- No coffee refill until the tool rack is sorted

- No checking personal messages until the equipment log is updated

- No podcast until the daily orders are packed and labeled

You're still saying "yes" to the reward – just on your terms, and not impulse's terms.

Step 4: Watch Internal Resistance Begin to Shrink

What makes this work so well for procrastination? Well:

- It turns delay into desire

- It frames discipline as trade, not deprivation

- It gives your brain a reason to push through discomfort

Over time, you're teaching yourself that *effort earns pleasure*, and that waiting doesn't mean never, *it just means later*.

This is how reflective delay becomes second nature, and procrastination steadily becomes less appealing than true accomplishment and progress.

IV: Build Task Immersion, Not Just Task Completion

If your mental ray is fixated on the end of the work... if it is too focused on the finish line, then every detail in the middle feels like a chore. You endlessly ponder over the result, dread the process, and ultimately end up delaying the start. Why? Because the middle part looks like a tunnel without light.

The answer, as such, isn't to push harder… it's to drop deeper into work itself.

Instead of asking: "*How fast can I do this?*"

Ask: "*How fully can I get into this right now?*"

Immersing yourself like this inspires a mental shift which then causes action to transition from *obligation to experience*.

Step 1: Read the "Why" of the Task Aloud

Procrastination feeds on disconnected tasks… tasks on your list that feel unrelated or arbitrary.

Take a moment to pause and read the reason aloud before starting on the task:

"*I'm cleaning this station to prep for tomorrow's shift.*"
"*I'm updating inventory because it avoids last-minute scrambles.*"
"*This task clears space for the big job ahead.*"

Articulating the why primes your brain to see the task as meaningful, and not just mandatory. It links effort to significance, which is a major antidote to avoidance and delay.

Step 2: Visualize the Task Being Done — Just for 10 Seconds

Close your eyes. Picture the completed task on your monitor. Picture sending it. Picture saving the file. The message written. The timetable made plain and clear, etc.

Don't get too carried away – 10 seconds is sufficient.

This conditions your brain with emotional closure in advance, before you've even begun. It creates a pull towards completion, as opposed to a push away from discomfort.

Step 3: Say Aloud: "I'm Entering the Task"... Then Name It

This small ritual is more significant than you might think.

By speaking, "I'm entering the task," you directly step into a stark shift in psychological posture – *away from avoidance and toward approach.*

Name it simply and clearly:

"I'm entering clean-up mode."
"I'm entering the supply check."
"I'm entering the end-of-day closeout."

That sentence – name it, claim it, enter it – directs your focus from ambient to focused, and becomes your door phrase to full mental immersion.

Step 4: Let Focus Be About Engagement, Not Output

Completion cannot be the only metric for success, and you must make a mental shift away from that ethos.

When the only win is being *done*, you'll resist anything that takes longer than expected (even if the extra time was absolutely necessary to use up).

But when success becomes *being fully engaged* – for a set time, with a full heart – procrastination steadily loses its grip.

You don't need to finish the whole thing anymore... you just need to be **in it**, *fully*, for now. And this needs to be your core philosophy, moving forward.

V: Use One-Tab, One-Task, One-Track Constraints

When your screen is cluttered, your mind follows suit.

Mental bandwidth is lost the instant ten tabs loom before you, notifications ping, multiple task lists compete for your attention, etc.

And while "discipline" may seem to be the obvious fix here, it really isn't. *Restrictions/constraints* are what actually make focus an easier option than distraction.

Let's walk through a constraint stack that will help fight overwhelm and restore mental clarity:

Step 1: One Tab Open – Max

Why it matters:

Every open tab is a "maybe."

Each one holds half-finished loops, unanswered questions, hidden context-switching prompts, etc. And that mental juggling creates a ton of lag and drag.

The fix: Use a one-tab rule on your Focus Block. One browser tab. One window. One attentional space, etc.

If you need another page? Open it in the background for a moment, do the action immediately, then close it and promptly return to your main tab.

Step 2: One Task Visible on Screen

Why it matters:

Split attention equals silent sabotage. Even if you're "focusing," your brain is nonetheless micro-processing every visible app, file, or open note.

Solution: *Hide everything else.*

Minimize or close unrelated windows. Pin one document, planner, or task app that holds the task at hand. Full-screen it if needed.

Having one clear window helps your brain step fully inside the work, rather than stand on the edge, looking at and assessing the twenty options laid out in front of it.

Step 3: One Audio Track on Repeat (If Any)

Why it matters:

Music may boost attention span – but novelty kills it. If you're following the lyrics in your mind, switching playlists, or reacting to fresh sounds, then *you're surreptitiously multitasking.*

Instead, listen to one instrumental track on repeat. Even better, listen to a track that your mind links with fierce work. Think of it as *an earworm anchor.*

It becomes a cue: *"When this song plays, I work."*

But what if music distracts you/is an attention deterrent? Well, try pure silence or white noise. Different things work for different people and what is more, focus and concentration do not necessarily need a soundtrack to thrive.

You've now learned how to herd distractions out of the way. The next challenge to tackle is *internal resistance.* The next chapter builds on the focus momentum we've built in this one by addressing what to do when motivation lags, even when/if you have the right systems and clarity already in place.

CHAPTER 18

MOTIVATE YOURSELF (EVEN WHEN YOU DON'T FEEL LIKE IT)

Motivation, as opposed to being something that you wait for, is something that you have to generate and build to establish and keep flowing. It's rarely ever the starting point by any means; it's almost always the outcome of consistent movement, clarity, and meaning. This chapter will teach you how to create the conditions that lead to a steady well of motivation, so that you're not waiting around to "feel ready" to get going/stop procrastinating.

Let's get to it.

I: Use Micro-Consequences to Activate Urgency

When you're dragging your feet, you shouldn't wait for motivation to show up. What needs doing, is to create urgency by putting small, immediate consequences or rewards on the table... at least just enough to get you in motion.

This has nothing to do with punishment by the way. The point of this is to spark and spur action when your inner motivation is low and procrastination is taking root.

Let's get it set up:

Step 1: Choose a Task that You're Putting Off

Pick one task that feels/has been stagnant – something you've been putting off, even though you know that it matters. Keep it bite-sized (e.g., write a paragraph, clean one shelf, send one email, etc.)

Write it down somewhere visible: Could be on a sticky note, a notepad, your to-do app, etc.

Example: *"Outline slide ideas for tomorrow's meeting."*

Step 2: Set a 5–10 Minute Action Window

Use your phone or a kitchen timer. This is the countdown window.

Then, attach a micro-stake:

- If I don't start this before the timer runs out, I miss my next coffee break.

- If I start now and work for 15 minutes, I earn 15 minutes of guilt-free scrolling later.

Make sure the reward or penalty is physical, immediate, and tied to a fun activity you enjoy or a dependency you have.

Step 3: Use a Physical Trigger to Lock It In

Create a ritual that marks the start:

- Place your phone out of reach (or into a drawer).

- Say out loud: "*I'm starting now.*"

- Open the app or document you'll be using… *and nothing else.*

This makes the transition from "intention" to "action" tactile and visible.

Step 4: Log It Briefly for Closure

Once done, jot down a quick win:

- *"Sent pitch email after 10-minute countdown"*

- *"Started slides, kept my reward break"*

Doing this instills follow-through not to mention it conditions your mind to associate effort with completion.

II: Turn Resistance into a Challenge Response

We pointed this out in the first part of the book (and at various points throughout): procrastination often begins with a low whisper. "I don't feel like it." "Let me just do this tomorrow." "I don't feel properly primed for this task." Etc. That voice is usually not necessarily dramatic – but it often is very insistent. However, understand that resistance shows up not to stop you, *but to see how you will respond.* And if you train the right reflex, *it's jet fuel for motivation.*

So, instead of viewing resistance as a reason to give up, view it as a challenge to try once more; a personal dare to respond with action.

Here's how to practice that shift in real-time:

Step 1: Record Your Resistance Scripts

Write down the exact language of your resistance for 1-2 days. Keep a running list. What is your brain saying to you right before you procrastinate?

Examples:

- *"I'm not in the zone."*
- *"This will take forever."*
- *"I'll just check this video/vine first."*

Doing this helps you view resistance as pattern, rather than truth. Once labeled, it ceases to have stealth power over you.

Step 2: Install a Challenge Phrase

Replace hesitation with a pre-thought-out reply. Something quick, direct, and action-oriented. Try:

- *"Let's go."*
- *"Bet."*
- *"What if I knock this segment right out the park?"*
- *"Watch me get started anyway."*

Use the same line each time to establish consistency.

Step 3: Create a Micro Challenge on the Spot

Give yourself something to pursue, *not just avoid*. Examples:

Examples:

- *"Let's see if I can clean out this bin before the clock hits :20."*
- *"Can I just tackle the wiring issue—nothing else right now?"*
- *"Let's out-focus my restlessness for the next 10 minutes."*

Pick something small, easy, and even slightly playful. The goal isn't to finish… showing up is all that needs doing.

Step 4: Track Challenge Wins, Not Just Finishes

Keep a "*Challenge Response Log*" in which you note every time you beat the moment of resistance – even if it's just a few minutes. It builds proof that *you can do it even when you don't feel like it.*

III: Leverage Social Presence — Even Without Involving People

Motivation often surges and spikes when someone is watching – or even when it merely feels like they might be. This isn't about people-pleasing, too; it's about tapping into a subtle, yet super-effective psychological stimulus: ambient accountability. What is more, you don't need a crowd or a coach… a strategic illusion of presence is enough to overcome procrastination inertia.

Let's build your solo-friendly support team:

Step 1: Try Body Doubling (With or Without Verbalization)

Body doubling is the act of working alongside someone else – even silently – to boost focus and follow-through.

Options:

- Join virtual co-working platforms like Focusmate[ii] or Flown[iii].

- Open a silent Zoom room with a friend (no conversation needed.)

- Play a "study with me" video on YouTube in another tab.

You may not be collaborating (collaborating isn't important/necessary anyway), but you're actively *sharing presence*, which will help anchor attention and reduce avoidance.

Step 2: Go Public with a Tiny Intentional Post

Declare your goal somewhere visible, even if it's just a temporary update:

- *"Today's focus: Clear shelf 3 and prep delivery stock. Update by 5 p.m."*

- *"First 25 minutes of tool maintenance begins now."*

Use social media, a group chat, or even your messaging status. You're not asking for accountability too… what you're doing is simulating exposure. The public nature boosts your internal follow-through.

Step 3: Send Yourself a Voice Note with a Commitment

Record a 15-second voice memo stating:

- What

- When

- Why

Play it back first, before getting started. Hearing your own voice – spoken with intent – creates a perscnal sort of "presence pressure" which sets follow-through in motion.

Example:

> *"Okay – one 30-minute inventory pass at 4:00 p.m. No interruptions. Time to close this open loop."*

IV: Borrow Motivation from a Future Version of You

When you find yourself stuck in the grip of procrastination, motivation can at times feel like it's on backorder. But there's a very easy mind hack to unlock urgency without anxiety: just imagine your Future Self – tomorrow's you.

And don't fantasize either… it is imperative that you imagine a realistic future version of yourself. Idealistic, for sure, but wholly tethered to reality nonetheless. The best thing about this, is that you get to decide how that future version of you feels – be it weighted by yet another undone thing (or series of undone things), or lighter, relieved, and *proud that you showed up today.*

Let's build that forward-leverage, step by step.

Step 1: Create a Mental Snapshot of Future You

Close your eyes for a second. Visualize:

- The end of today or tomorrow morning.

- You having finished only one major portion of what you're procrastinating on doing right now.

Ask yourself:

- *"How would that version of me feel?"*

- *"What would I be free to work on?"*

The goal here, is to borrow the sense of eventual, future relief and *apply it directly as motivation for action, now*.

Step 2: Use the Thank-You Prompt

Ask:

> *"What would Future Me thank me for doing right now?"*

Don't think in terms of big goals. Think:

- Sprucing up those loose ends in the project

- Making that overdue client pitch

- Starting that 15-minute session

Example: *"Thanks for not putting this micro-task off again. It feels nice knowing we're not waking up dreading about it tomorrow."*

This small bit of dialogue rephrases your present action *as an act of self-kindness*, and not a punishment.

Step 3: Write a 2-Line Message from Future You

Optional, but effective. Write down:

- Line 1: What you did.

- Line 2: Why it worked.

Example:

> *"You edited those three slides. This puts us ahead by quite a margin, and my brain feels 10 pounds lighter."*

Stick it on a post-it, phone note, or say it aloud. Doing this makes accountability personal, and brings purpose into the moment.

When you really mull over it, it becomes apparent that your biggest motivator isn't the thing that fires you up; rather, it's the empathy from the version of yourself that stands to *benefit from assertive action today*. So, *use it*.

V: Create an Energizing Language Loop

Words don't just describe your experience… they actually shape it and coax it into 3D as well. The words you say to yourself in your mind can shrivel you up before you even begin… or they can ignite your energy and motion in a way that few other things can.

When procrastination kicks in, your self-talk often goes along the following lines:

- *"I have to do this."*
- *"This is going to suck."*
- *"Ugh, I'm already behind."*

This kind of language forms a loop... one that drains motivation before action even starts. But with some quick rewrites, you can form a new loop that *charges up instead of binds*.

Here's how to do it.

Step 1: Catch the Draining Language in Real-Time

Start by noticing the language you use immediately before procrastinating on a task. Some common energy-zapping triggers include:

- *"I have to..."*
- *"This is going to be hard."*
- *"I'm not feeling like it."*

Write those down over a few days. Complete awareness of them is the first step towards their revision and overhaul.

Step 2: Build Your Personal Reframes List

Replace every draining statement with a substitute that *opens the door to action instead of slamming it shut*.

Examples:

- "I have to write this" → "*I get to move this project forward*."
- "This is hard" → "*This is challenge training. Let's see how I handle it.*"
- "I don't feel like it" → "*Let me just get it moving. There's no pressure to finish right here and now, anyway.*"

Make 3-5 of your own reframes and keep them within easy access; on a sticky note, home-screen, or notebook perhaps.

Step 3: Say It Before You Start, Not Later

The loop only works *when it segues into action*.

Right before beginning a task:

- Read or say your reframed line aloud

- Tap it with a little physical reminder (e.g., hand on table, inhale)

By doing this, you're effectively choosing a lens that gives you energy, not dread/anxiety/overwhelm.

VI: Use Visual Progress Feedback to Motivate Ongoing Action

Progress doesn't just feel good… it's great fuel for motivation as well. But here's the catch: your brain doesn't always register how far you've come *unless it can see it*.

That's why visual feedback tools are powerful. They don't just track what's done; they also track and show momentum in a way that keeps procrastination at bay. When progress is visible, *your next action feels easier to justify and emotionally satisfying to take*.

Let's build your visual momentum system.

Step 1: Choose a Visual Tracking Format That Works for Your Particular Style

You don't need an expensive app. You just need a clean and simple visual. Choose a format based on your workflow:

- Checklists (digital or written): satisfying and quick to tick off

- Progress bars (manual or auto): great for large projects

- Kanban or column boards (e.g., "To Do," "Doing," "Done")

- Color-coded calendars: mark off days/tasks completed with a glance

Tip: If it feels clunky, you won't stick with it. *Keep it lean and visible.*

Step 2: Make Your Progress Board Unmissable

Place your tracker in a location where you'll see it every day, and not buried in a folder or app tab. Examples:

- A wall chart on the wall next to your workspace

- A digital widget on your computer or phone desktop

- A whiteboard that you fill in each night

Visibility is the key. Out of sight = out of motivation.

Step 3: Log Movement, Not Just Completion

Don't just log complete tasks; log progress milestones too:

- *"Sent out 50 invoices" counts*

- *"Did 1 Pomodoro" counts*

- *"Sketched out the plan" counts*

This earns *emotional credit* for being here, not merely finishing.

Step 4: Look Back Weekly to Reflect and Refuel

At the end of the week, take 5 minutes looking back at what drummed up momentum. Ask yourself:

- *"What am I proud I stuck with?"*
- *"What momentum can I carry forward?"*

That little habit fuels progress, not to mention it diminishes the fear of starting over.

Procrastination thrives on invisibility. Get your work out in the open, and your willpower shows too.

The thing with motivation is that, like with many other things, it doesn't appear out of nowhere – it responds to *action*, *purpose*, and *perspective*. When you move, reframe, and reconnect, motivation follows. There's no need to chase or force it. You just need to create the conditions where it naturally arrives. As in, *open the door – and let motivation walk in.*

With motivation tools in place, it's now time to *organize everything* into a weekly system. The playbook, explored in the next chapter, gives you a framework to put all the hard-won procrastination-eliminating skills that you've picked up thus far *into consistent weekly execution.*

CHAPTER 19

YOUR PRODUCTIVITY PLAYBOOK

A productivity playbook is not a to-do list. It's a functional, self-authored cheat sheet... something to move you to act even when your head is foggy, your mood is awful, and procrastination is quietly, but incessantly, whispering its usual excuses.

Think of it as your own operations guide: quick-reference guidelines for how you function best, *in the areas of life most significant to you.*

When procrastination comes knocking yet again (and best believe it always will), the playbook will lead the charge at the frontlines... so you won't have to think your way repeatedly out of inertia again.

Let's get started.

I: Why a Playbook is Effective

1. It Minimizes Friction

Procrastination, a lot of the times, stems from micro-frictions.

- *"Where do I begin?"*
- *"What do I do?"*
- *"What's the best way to do this?"*

Your playbook answers those questions in advance, so that action *becomes more straightforward and less difficult than deferment/delay.*

2. It Shatters Overthinking Loops

Indecision is procrastination's best friend. A playbook *is a set of clear decisions put together well ahead of time*: when motivation is low or energy is drained, you run through the script you wrote *while you were in a good place.*

3. It Preserves Your Smart Moves

When you're at your best, you have a proper grasp on how you work and perform: *what time of day you're most productive, how to reach flow state, when to reel it in*, etc. But we often forget, especially when both environment and mood are less than ideal. The playbook retains this information so that the bothered/troubled version of you that wants to quit can access can reboot and re-launch.

4. It Guides Action When You're in Low-Motivation States

Motivation may fail you, but systems will not. A playbook gives you *backup frameworks*, *default routines*, and *quick-start practices* when your willpower runs out.

II: Identify Your High-Impact Zones

A productivity system can't be one-size-fits-all, and this is because the whole scope of your life also isn't like that at all. The quickest way to waste effort? *Spreading it evenly on everything.*

Instead, you need to focus your efforts into those aspects where *productivity matters most.*

Let's determine your High-Impact Zones; the *3-5 High-Priority areas of life* where traction is most critical.

Step 1: Write down the Key Domains of your current life

Do a quick, zero-judgment inventory of what fills your weeks. Put it in terms of domains or spheres, *not tasks*:

- Professional (e.g., Deep Work, Admin, Client Management)

- Personal (e.g., Family Logistics, Health, Finances)

- Growth (e.g., Learning, Side Projects, Creative Work)

Example: As a startup founder, you might have: 1) Product Strategy, 2) Team Management, 3) Personal Health, 4) Reading & Thinking Time.

Step 2: Ask: Where Does Progress Actually Matter?

Not all zones are worth optimizing. Call out the few where relentless effort creates disproportionate results… *where procrastination hurts the most and progress compounds.*

Ask:

- *Where do I feel procrastination's pinch most?*
- *Which zones lead to real-life consequences if I procrastinate?*
- *Where would small, consistent victories significantly change outcomes?*

Example: As a software programmer, you may see that procrastination in "Career Development" (i.e., applying to new jobs) leads to more long-term regret than putting off chores – *so that zone gets first priority*.

Step 3: Identify 3-5 High-Impact Zones as Your Playbook Focus

Put these zones into writing. They are the sole spots that your playbook *must streamline*. No need to organize every little aspect of your entire life.

Tag them clearly:

- Zone 1: Deep Work – strategic problem-solving
- Zone 2: Admin & Execution – completing the projects
- Zone 3: Personal Recovery – sleep, food, relaxation

This clarity turns your productivity system from a one-size-fits-all to-do list into a *customized set of tools* built to serve your real goals, and *not your guilt*.

III: Choose Your Signature Work Modes

You don't need to copy and clone productivity hacks that were never designed specifically for you in the first place. It's okay to take bits here and there from the general-use templates you'll find in the internet, but what you really need is your own schedule – a *Focus Profile*, so to speak – of when and how your brain works best.

The more you understand your natural work modes, the less you'll struggle to get started and keep things moving. This is because you're able to surf your own current instead of (unwittingly) trying to swim against it.

Let's build up that profile.

Step 1: Define Your Natural High-Performance Windows

Start by defining when you function at your best, and both mind and motion are at their most optimal. Note that these windows do not point to when you are present/free/obligated to work… they point to when your mind and body are best primed for task execution. We already highlighted this earlier, so there's no need to go over it in close detail once more. But it's a very valid step here, so we'll include it.

Example: *"8:30–11:00 AM = Deep Focus," "3–5 PM = admin/light tasks," "post-8 PM = off-limits."*

Bonus: *Look for trends over the week. Maybe Tuesday mornings are fresher than Mondays.*

Step 2: Define Your Ideal Focus Burst Lengths

Not everyone performs best on 25-minute Pomodoros or 90-minute marathons, or whatever else the gurus out there preach and market. We're all different in our own ways.

Experiment and jot down your own sweet spot:

- How long can I work before I need a mental reset?

- What feels challenging but manageable?

Sample: "*I find my groove at 45-minute blocks with 5–10 min breaks. Two blocks maximum before I need a longer reset.*"

This is your default rhythm, not a rule. It eliminates procrastination by reducing uncertainty over how long to work.

Step 3: Map Your Optimal Environment Settings

Finally, define your most distraction-free and energizing setup.

Consider:

- Ambient sound: silent? gentle music? white noise?

- Physical space: open area? corner desk? coffee shop?

- Input blockers: Do Not Disturb? airplane mode? headphones?

Example: "*Noise-canceling headphones, one-tab browser, warm light, and no phone in sight.*"

The goal is not to create a dream environment, but to understand what does work for you – so that even a half-way match gives you a stronger launch platform.

IV: Build Your "Action Protocols"

When you're low on energy, sidetracked, or out of your mojo, it's difficult to know where to start – or when to stop. That's where *Action Protocols* come in.

Think of them as mini-playbooks for each significant part of your life. They eliminate procrastination *by eliminating guesswork*. Each protocol spells out answers for the following batched questions:

What motivates you into action, what keeps you going, and how do you finish neatly?

Let's build yours.

Step 1: Choose a Zone to Protocolize

Pick one of your High-Impact Zones… particularly one that you are prone to procrastinating or stumbling over.

Examples:

- Deep Work (creative work, planning, writing)
- Admin (email, bills, errands)
- Learning (reading, online learning)
- Fitness (home exercise, gym, walk)

Start with just one. Don't over-engineer.

Step 2: Define the 4-Part Protocol Structure

1. Trigger – The ritual or cue that begins the zone
   → *"When I make coffee + wear headphones, I initiate Deep Work."*

2. Setup – The specific environment or tool configuration
   → *"I open my client doc, activate one playlist, and close all unnecessary tabs."*

3. First Action – A low-pressure, frictionless initiator
   → *"I write one throwaway paragraph or brainstorm five ideas."*

4. Exit Strategy – A clean, satisfying end
   → *"I log what's done in Notion and leave a 1-sentence next step."*

This gives your brain a familiar sequence. Less hesitation. Less decision fatigue.

Step 3: Write and Save It Where You'll Use It

Don't just leave your protocol in your head. Store it visibly as well:

- Pin it to your workspace

- Add it to the top of your digital project files

- Print it next to your calendar

Example Protocol: Admin Zone

Trigger: Stretch + glass of water

Setup: Open task tracker, email inbox minimized

First Action: Clear two flagged messages

Exit Strategy: Mark what's pending + shut browser

Repeat this process for 2–3 zones. When procrastination flares up, you'll have a proven runway that will help you launch regardless of how unideal conditions and mood are.

V: Define Your "Disruption Recovery Moves"

Even when you have the best productivity system, life will at times interfere and knock you off-track. The problem, by the way, isn't the interruption itself, since this is inevitable – it's not having a backup plan in place. That's usually when procrastination kicks in under the guise of "*I'll start over later.*"

To stay consistent, you need fallback plays: default habits that allow you to recover, refocus, and return with ease.

These aren't plan B, by any means... what they are, are *resilience tools*.

Let's build yours.

Step 1: Identify Your 3 Most Common Disruption Scenarios

Everyone has personal weak points. Find yours.

Examples:

- Being mentally foggy or emotionally flat
- Missing a scheduled work block or routine
- Being overwhelmed by new requirements or task piles

Don't guess, either. Reflect on the latest 2-3 occasions on which your flow broke. *What happened exactly*? Log this.

Step 2: Create Your Recovery Response Prompts

Now fill in a statement-based playbook with these templates:

- "When I feel stuck, I…"
  → "*…perform a 5-minute brain dump to clear noise.*"

- "When I've missed a day, I…"
  → " *… get back on track with a 'light version' of the habit-half the time, same focus.*"

- "When I feel overwhelmed, I…"
  → "*… categorize tasks into 3 piles: Must-Do / Can Wait / Delete.*"

Far from being motivational mantras, these are *actionable steps* that you can execute immediately.

Step 3: Make Your Recovery Protocol Visible and Usable

Put your three recovery moves where you can easily see them when you're off-track:

- On a sticky note on your desk

- Pinned to the top of your digital notes' app

- As a daily reminder on your phone

Example:

Disruption Recovery Card

When I am stuck → write a rough, functional draft, not a perfect one.

When I skip → restart with a small task.

When overwhelmed → exercise, breathe, then re-prioritize list.

You don't need to eliminate all disturbance. *You just need to know what to do next when it shows up.*

That's how you stop procrastination from becoming a singular fissure that snowballs into a collapse.

VI: Keep It Visible, Adaptable, and Alive

Your productivity playbook is only effective *if you implement it.*

Far too many people write excellent systems that would take them places if they applied them… and then set them aside in a folder to collect virtual dust. The result? You inevitably just end up slipping back into old habits, and procrastination gets back on schedule.

To prevent that, your playbook has to *stay visible, stay in action, and stay personal to you.*

Here's how to do it.

Step 1: Make It "Frictionless-ly" Visible

If you can't see it, you won't use it. As such, you need to settle on a format that *reflects your real-world behavior.*

Options:

- Print a one-page at-a-glance summary and place it on your wall, desk, or mirror.

- Save a quick reference version as your phone's wallpaper lock screen.

- Add an instant-access tab or shortcut to your browser home bar.

- Set up a weekly recurring reminder that opens your digital playbook document.

Have it in a place where you're sure to bump into it every day.

Step 2: Schedule a Monthly Review Ritual

A dormant system is as every bit just as bad as having no system in place. To prevent ending up with a dormant system, set up a monthly recurring calendar event... a 15-minute check-in, so to speak.

Ask:

- What worked well in the playbook this month?

- Where did I still fall into delay or decision fatigue?

- What one adjustment would make the system more usable next month?

This keeps your system responsive, and not rigid.

Example: You realize your "Focus Block" habit is too long on Fridays, so you cut it back by 30 minutes or so. That small adjustment keeps you consistent instead of disillusioned every time you stumble.

Step 3: Let Utility Trump Perfection

Don't wait until your playbook looks pretty enough. Pretty is overrated. Focus on making it as functional as possible.

Your playbook is not a Pinterest board... it's your own anti-procrastination toolbox. Aim for "*good enough to use*," not "*pretty enough to frame/flex with to my friends*.".

Also, remember to update it as your priorities change, and allow it to change as your habits get steadily tighter and more refined.

With this covered, the next chapter introduces non-punitive, minimalist tracking methods to help you track your progress without falling into obsessive self-judgment or burnout. It reframes measurement as *awareness*, not accountability, and will cover tools like micro-journaling, trend-spotting, and habit reflections that support long-term consistency without stress.

CHAPTER 20

MEASURE WITHOUT PRESSURE

Tracking often starts with the finest of intentions... but then all too often, it rapidly spirals into guilt. A singular missed goal balloons into self-criticism and avoidance, and so on and so forth, and everything unravels from there. The problem isn't the measurement in itself... it's the anxiety we sprinkle onto it. This chapter focuses on using measurement as a gentle guide, *and not a grade*.

Observe, don't criticize. Adjust, don't shame.

Let's get to it.

I: The Three Types of Measurement (And Which One to Focus On)

If you wish to overcome procrastination in the long term, you need to track your progress... but not how everybody else typically goes about it.

Most procrastinators either don't track progress at all (because they're afraid of what they'll see), or, as we'd highlighted before, track only one factor: quantity. That's a trap, especially because productivity, more than being just about quantity, is about *consistency* and *awareness* as well. In fact, these two latter metrics are far, far more important and impactful as far as productivity goes, than quantity could ever hope to be.

Let's break them down.

1. Quantitative Output (How much did you do?)

This is the default metric. It tracks your raw numbers:

- Micro-tasks completed

- Calls made

- Hours logged

- Invoices sent

While useful, this type of measurement often fuels guilt and burnout; especially if you're behind. As someone prone to procrastination, obsessing over output creates pressure loops that can backfire.

As such, only use this sparingly. *Never* lead with it.

2. Behavioral Consistency (Did you show up today?)

This is procrastinators' gold standard.

Rather than track how much you accomplished, *track whether you did the behavior*:

- Did I start stacking/unloading my shop shelves at 9:00?

- Did I open the project?

- Did I complete my 25-min block of concentration?

Small regular wins create self-trust, not to mention they shrink avoidance over time.

Track this every day. A checkbox will do.

3. Qualitative Self-Awareness (How did it feel? What worked?)

This one's criminally underutilized, especially given how potent it is.

After a session, ask:

- What worked?

- What didn't work?

- What made it easier or harder?

This kind of reflection helps you hone your system and actually get it to work for you, which is the secret to long-term progress.

Log 1-2 brief notes after a work block or weekly review.

II: Build a Weekly "Self-Observation Loop"

Progress only sticks if you pay attention to it. And procrastination only breaks if you make a habit of catching it.

That's where a weekly *Self-Observation Loop* comes in. Think of it as a gentle check-in that helps you observe your patterns without judgment. Not a performance review, and most certainly not a visit to the guilt station. Just a chance to halt, observe, and *get better*.

Let's get to it:

Step 1: Choose a Weekly Check-in Window

Pick a consistent time to reflect: Friday afternoon, Sunday evening, Monday morning, etc. Make it quick (10-15 minutes max) and link it to a stimulus (coffee, calendar check, work session end, etc.)

Hint: The routine is more important than the time you pick. *Pick a time that you can stick to*, whatever it is.

Step 2: Use the "3–1–1" Observation Template

To keep it simple and non-intimidating, use this light-touch template:

- 3 Wins – What did it feel like you made progress on, no matter how small?

  (Example: "*Sent that invoice I'd been putting off. Did a 20-min workout twice. Made 7 calls to prospective clients for my start-up.*")

- 1 Lesson – What did you learn about how you work?

  (Example: "*I procrastinate on tasks if I don't pivot as swiftly as possible from one activity to the other, once the time comes to make the shift.*")

- 1 Adjustment – What's one thing I need to adjust next week?

  (Example: "*I'll have my to-do list ready before I log off each day.*")

This format keeps the loop short, focused, and actionable.

Step 3: Notice Patterns of Avoidance (Without Judgment)

Gently ask yourself every week:

- *"Where did I stop or avoid?"*
- *"What made the moment clunky?"*
- *"What got me moving anyway?"*

By recording what got you moving, you build your own effective, knowledge-grounded anti-procrastination playbook over time.

III: Design a "Non-Comparative Dashboard"

Procrastination feeds on comparison. You scroll, compare, feel behind… and then you find yourself unable to start. Not because the task is too big, or too nuanced, but because *your own self-worth is too caught up in how everyone else is doing it better*.

This is why you need a *Non-Comparative Dashboard*: a personal, self-referential system tracking your own inputs and experiences… and *NOT anyone else's output*.

No benchmarks. No likes. No fake races.

Let's set yours up:

Step 1: Measure Consistency, Not Quantity

Start with the most important metric for the procrastinator: *Did I show up*?

Create a simple tracker – checkbox, app, or notebook – marking whether you worked in each key zone (e.g., repairs, admin, training, client calls, etc.) for each day or week.

Don't track how much. *Track if.*

Example: "*Spent 20 mins on website*" is a win. Even if you didn't finish.

Step 2: Log Emotional Friction Scores

Add an internal scale: *How resistant was I?*

Scale your resistance 1-5 after each task session:

- 1 = Gliding, no resistance
- 3 = Gentle pushback, but I can manage
- 5 = Heavy dread, strong avoidance

You'll develop your own patterns, by and by, and you'll gradually understand which tasks drain you – and when especially this is the case. This prevents you from blaming your willpower by default, like we so often do, and instead allow you to redesign your approach so you can keep plugging away.

Step 3: Create Custom Progress Checkpoints

Instead of striving for flawless results, ask yourself: Did I work on this meaningfully?

Use your own queries:

- *"Did I start when I said I would?"*

- *"Did I actually do the task – not it's substitute?"*
- *"Did I leave it clearer and more applicable than I found it?"*

This kind of monitoring builds self-trust all while undercutting the scourge of self-blame.

IV: Create Low-Stakes Progress Markers

We highlighted this particular point before as well: for most procrastinators, the biggest thing standing in the way of starting is the belief that anything less than a home run is a swing and a miss. And when the standard is so high, *effort is for naught unless it is perfect.* That perfectionism feeds paralysis.

Low-stakes markers of progress: simple, flexible measures that track momentum, *not milestones.*

You're not compromising… rather, you're *reframing success so you can start again.*

Step 1: Count the Initiation, Not the Outcome

Begin by rewarding yourself for appearing, rather than completing.

- *"I opened the spreadsheet"*
- *"I set a 15-minute timer"*
- *"I read yesterday's notes"*

These movements may feel insignificant, but they're very effective in snapping the inertia cycle. And that is the real victory as someone prone to procrastination. Make it a daily habit to track these micro-launches, even if the session didn't have a sense of being "productive."

Step 2: Build a Personal Progress Chain

Forget streaks based on perfection. Instead, ask yourself: Did I engage today, even just by a bit?

Use a simple tracker (calendar, bullet journal, app) and mark a ✓ if you interacted with your habit or task. The aim isn't what you did, *but that you did something.*

Miss a day? Start again without guilt. Progress chains are about consistency, more than anything else.

Step 3: Rate Your Internal Experience

Each day or session, write down a quick check-in

- Confidence Score (1-5): *How in control did I feel?*

- Simplicity Meter (✓/X): *Did I make the path to the task simpler?*

These soft measures enable you to keep tabs on your system's health, not just your to-do list.

V: Use Measurement as a Form of Self-Compassion

For many of us who are prone to procrastinating, "tracking" often feels like surveillance. A scoreboard. A way to confirm you're behind, almost. But when used with the right mindset, measurement ceases to be hinged on pressure and instead gets centered on establishing partnership with your future self.

Think of it as *self-compassion in spreadsheet form.* You're not measuring to push harder; *you're measuring to understand better.*

Done right, tracking becomes a quiet act of support: a tool for reducing friction, and not a shame amplifier.

Step 1: Ask, "What Would Help Future Me?"

Before taking a look and reviewing a task log, habit streak, weekly dashboard, etc., do take a moment to ask yourself:

> "*If I were trying to make life easier for Future Me, what would I want to know right now?*"

Doing this effectively shifts tracking *from judgment to compassion.*

For example:

- If you notice you always skip workouts on Tuesdays, the solution isn't "be more disciplined." It's "*Tuesdays are tight... perhaps I can juggle things around?*"

- If your energy is depleted at 3 p.m., don't put that down as a failure. Mark it down as a signal: "*This is where I need an easier task or a break.*"

Step 2: Use Data to Lighten the Load

Once you've gathered rough-and-ready data – streaks, energy levels, points of friction, et al – ask:

- What does this tell me I need to do less of?
  (e.g., long blocks of work following lunch, too many open commitments on Mondays)

- Where can I cut friction?

  (e.g., prepare my work files the night before, automate common admin tasks)

Let your data feel relieving, not rebuking.

Step 3: Choose Tracking That Feels Like Support

Choose low-pressure formats:

- *"What felt heavy today?"*
- *"What made things smoother?"*
- *"What would I do differently – kindly?"*

When your measurements *communicate inquiry instead of judgment*, your system becomes sustainable, and sustainable systems are very effective at dissolving procrastination.

This is what the Compassionate Tracker practices: Less bullwhip, and more mirror-held-with-gentle-care.

VI: Know When to Stop Measuring and Just Live

Measurement is a means, *not an end*. It's meant to *augment your attention, not consume it*. At some point, measurement needs to fade into the background and let life take the wheel.

As someone who's susceptible to bouts of procrastination, you might do well with soft data to help build momentum and sear confidence into your psyche. But sooner or later, if you're not careful, measurement does tend to devolve into micromanagement. *And that's exactly when you need to call a halt* to it.

Progress isn't constant analysis. Progress is believing that you've gathered enough, and believing in yourself enough to the point where you live the habit, as opposed to just tracking it.

Step 1: Watch for Diminishing Returns

The very first sign that it's time to let go?

You're tracking, *but it's no longer revealing anything new to you.*

Perhaps, you're tracking your daily reading habit, but have already arrived at the point where you already know that you're consistent. Perhaps you're logging mood scores, but they've been stable for a while.

If your insights have flattened, then measurement has succeeded and is no longer necessary. You do not have to keep inquiring about the same things once you have learned the response.

Step 2: Notice When It's Becoming a Source of Pressure

Measurement should reduce resistance, NOT create it.

Ask yourself:

- *"Am I logging this because it helps… or because I feel guilty if I don't?"*
- *"Is this system keeping me involved… or driving me crazy?"*

If your habit tracker is a drag, that's your signal to drop it. Don't trade one type of procrastination (avoidance) for another (compulsive checking).

Step 3: Create a Trust-Based Off-Ramp

Here's your permission slip:

When you've developed solid rhythms – stop tracking them.

You don't need to track brushing your teeth, now, do you? Same goes for any habit that now feels natural.

Let the playbook evolve. Then archive the tracker and close the tab.

This, at its core, *is maturity*. After all, the goal of pretty much every support system made by man *is to ultimately become unnecessary*. When you've internalized the rhythm, live it freely. You don't need to keep dipping back in for proof… it's no longer required at this point.

Now that this is in order, the next step is to help you identify *subtle, recurring drains* – people-pleasing, indecision, open loops, low-level anxiety, you name it – that sabotage productivity from the shadows. Chapter 21 explores this comprehensively.

CHAPTER 21

KILL THE HIDDEN DRAINS ON PROGRESS

Sometimes, even when you are showing up like you know you should and doing everything in your power to get the work accomplished, things still feel off... slow, heavy, fuzzy, etc. When this is the case, it all too often is the consequence of hidden drains that you need to bring up to the surface and then promptly plug: *subtle habits, assumptions, or obligations sneakily draining your energy*. This chapter is about discovering those unseen leaks, and sealing them so your effort actually drives you forward.

Let's get to it.

I: Drain #1: Micro-Indecision

Procrastination often sneaks in through micro-indecisions. These micro-indecisions are tiny mental stalls that, once bunched up and chained, pin you down and quietly erode your momentum.

Look at them this way:

You think you're just "taking a second" to decide…

Whether to start now or in 10 minutes.

Which draft to revise first.

If something is polished enough to hit send.

Etc.

But these momentary stalls tend to pile up, clog your mental bandwidth, and feed the familiar delay loop of "I'll come back to this later." Later then becomes tomorrow, and tomorrow ultimately becomes never.

The problem here is decision fatigue, more than anything. And the solution, as should be all too apparent by now, is not trying to generate more willpower – it's creating pre-decisions to your counter micro-indecisions, and embedding them firmly.

Here's how to go about it:

Step 1: Identify Your Repeat Friction Points

Start by bringing the micro-indecisions that routinely catch you off guard into the light. Track your workday for a day and log:

- When do you unnecessarily stall?

- What questions habitually repeat themselves?

- Where do you "stall for clarity" but never really get any?

Example

You have a habit of sitting down and asking yourself, "What should I do first?" That is a decision that can be made once – not necessarily every passing day.

Step 2: Install Simple Defaults

Default rules create auto-answers to routine indecision traps.

Examples include:

- "Default to done"
  → Send the email when it's 85% good.

- "Start with the shortest"
  → For messy lists, do the quickest item first.

- "If I'm unsure, I start anyway"
  → Clarity comes mid-motion.

Make them your working rules. Write them down. Say them out loud and allow them to override the spiral.

Step 3: Use a "Decision Protocol" Cheat Sheet

Develop a personal playbook of go-to responses for your top 3-5 most common questions. For example:

- "What if I'm not ready?"
  → "Set the timer for 10 minutes anyway."

- "Do what project first?"
  → "Do the one that's nearest done."

- "What if I'm thinking too much?"
  → "Ship it. Fix later."

As soon as your brain gets used to the rule, it no longer hesitates or asks for active mental input, and momentum is able to kick in.

Micro-decisions shrink when they're no longer yours to actively make all the time.

II: Drain #2: Loose Commitments

Loose commitments are mental leeches of the worst kind. They look and sound harmless –mere fuzzy ideas floating in your mental background – but they really drain clarity, focus, and energy by pretending to be priorities.

You've probably heard (or are perhaps even presently hearing) the following voices in your head:

- "I kind of want to start that side project…"
- "I should probably help with that team thing…"
- "I've been meaning to get back to that idea…"

The problem is that none of these are solid. None have deadlines. *But they all take up space.*

Left un-cured, they drain your brain. You end up always thinking about them, but never doing anything about them since there's no viable action map for them. That very indecision propels procrastination, since you end up getting weighed down by what you have not (and cannot) decide yet.

Step 1: Surface the Vague Stuff

Take five minutes and take a "loose commitment dump." Write down all projects, goals, or commitments that are in the "maybe," "someday," or "I should" category.

Don't censor anything either; let it all out.

Now, scan your list. How many of these are things that you've perhaps half-committed to but haven't properly defined?

Those are your drains.

Step 2: Make a Binary Decision – In or Out

For each thing, ask:

- Am I really committed to this?

- Would I be relieved if it vanished?

If no, ditch it. You don't have to keep it on life support. Erase it. Say no. *Decline politely but firmly.*

If yes, excellent – but it's time to stop faffing around and go all in.

Step 3: If "In," Define the Next Step. If "Out," Let It Go Entirely

For each item you're keeping, write down the very next concrete action. Not the entire plan; just the next step.

- "Draft the client pitch outline"

- "Book a 20-min research slot"

- "Buy the domain"

For what you're dropping, *make it official*. Archive it, remove it from your task list, or close the tab. Do not, by any means, let it hover.

Loose commitments, as we mentioned, are mental leeches of the worst kind and as such, you have to make the call to either *commit or clear*. Nothing in between.

III: Drain #3: Unspoken Resentments

Some of the largest drains on your focus aren't technical, logistical, or even explicit. They're emotional… and they're often unstated.

Hidden frustrations almost always tend to simmer beneath the surface, bothering you, weighing down your psyche and quietly draining your motivation. They buzz – quietly but persistently – stealing your energy, patience, and motivation.

You might be:

- Fed up that a colleague never pulls their own share of the weight.

- Bitter that your efforts go unrewarded.

- Seething at yourself for missed chances, lost time, or habitual procrastination.

These internal struggles don't just make you feel awful… they stall you as well, and the unspoken anger stemming from them becomes dense static that all blocks forward progress. A lot of the time, you avoid and delay not because the task at hand is hard, but because you're too emotionally murky to chain successive forward steps.

Let's put this drain behind us.

Step 1: Write Out the Resentment

Take five minutes. No editing. No tact. Just write:

- "I'm still mad at ___ for ___."

- "I'm mad that I always ___."

- "I wish ___ could have turned out otherwise."

Don't judge it. Don't try to solve it yet. *Just name it*.

It's not very possible to clear that which you haven't identified yet.

Step 2: Decide: Act, Release, or Reframe

Check what you've written. For each resentment, choose to do one of three things:

- Act: Do it. Say it. Stop it.

- Release: If it's trivial or stale, release it. Say it aloud: "*This is no longer worth my energy*."

- Reframe: Alter the lens. Rather than "*They always take me for granted*," say "*I'm entitled to say no more often*."

Step 3: Take One Small Closure Step

Pick one resentment and move toward closure:

- "Write up the message/client pitch and wrap it up (even if you don't send it).

- Get rid of something tied to a past version of yourself.

- Permission-slip yourself and get on with it, regardless of whether the result is imperfect.

Unspoken resentment are glue traps. Vent them. Work through them and release the energy that they've been holding hostage.

IV: Drain #4: Half-Open Loops

Your brain is too creative, dynamic and useful device to just be a passive container for your thoughts, ideas and whims. It's meant for active thinking, not dormant storing. That's the reason half-open loops... tasks, conversations, or decisions you've started but never finished, suck energy out of you *without you even realizing it...* because it's against your brain's nature to just store them up passively. And so, it keeps going right back to them, picking and prodding at them and burning mental energy and capacity as a result.

Think of each one as being like an open tab in your mental browser, siphoning off attention and eating away at the RAM, even when/though you're not actively thinking about it.

Examples of half-open loops:

- You started composing a client pitch but never sent it.

- You committed to a friend that you'd "soon" get back to them but didn't.

- You began working on a project and left it hanging, uncommitted, and uncategorized.

These piles of incomplete tasks tend to generate ambient tension in the background. They also don't just clutter your calendar; they also clutter your head, and make even the most mundane things feel significantly heavier

It's high time you closed these loops.

Step 1: Audit Your Open Loops

Get a timer set to 15–20 minutes and ask yourself:

- *"What have I started and not finished?*
- *"Where have I done a follow-up and not followed through?"*
- *"What to-dos or projects are hanging without next steps?"*

Jot them down… don't solve them yet. Just bring them to the surface and acknowledge them as your active drains.

Step 2: Apply the 3C Rule – Close, Calendar, or Cancel

For each loop, decide:

- Close it – If it will take under 10 minutes, just do it now.
- Calendar it – If it's important but needs time, schedule a definite slot for it.
- Cancel it – If it doesn't matter any longer, intentionally let it go. Archive the document. Say "no" out loud. Cross it out.

Step 3: Create a Loop Review Ritual

On a weekly basis, look for any new loops that are in the process of forming. If they have been open for more than 7-10 days, run them through the 3C filter again.

Your mind craves clarity. As such, open loops create delay while closed loops create momentum.

V: Drain #5: Default Association with Draining People

Not every drain is on your calendar. If you really assess things, you'll find that some of the worst ones *are in the company that you keep.*

We're not talking about cutting off toxic people either... we're talking about recognizing when you've defaulted into too much time with mismatched energy; people whose presence every so subtly chips away at your motivation.

Also, chances are high that none of these folks are malicious. Still, they might be:

- Emotionally chaotic
- Chronically negative or cynical
- Constantly needy or attention-hungry
- Unfocused, reactive, or addicted to distraction

Over time, this subtle dissonance rewires your own mind. You catch their tempo. You absorb their (often unwarranted and perhaps aimless) sense of urgency. You absorb their tension. And this ends up making progress more work than it has any right to be.

Let's fix that.

Step 1: Recognize the Energy Mismatch

Ask yourself:

- "Who leaves me more stressed or low-energy after we hang out together?"

- "Who do I find myself defaulting to hanging out with, rather than doing it by choice?"

- "Who drains my energy even when we're just talking about nothing in particular?"

Create a personal, judgment-free list, and think about all this as being about guarding your productivity, first and foremost, as opposed to leveling judgment on others.

Step 2: Create Contact Boundaries

You don't need to disappear… you just need *to not always be on and available*.

- Limit spontaneous access: Disable read receipts. Disable auto-replies. Delay non-essential callbacks.

- Shift to low-bandwidth formats: Text instead of calling. Async messages instead of the in-the-moment rants.

- Schedule contact with intention: If you do want to keep someone in your life, set time limits. Don't let them spill over into your most productive energy times.

Step 3: Incorporate Intentional Recharge Time

After high-drain interactions, *add a mindful recovery activity*:

- A calm walk

- 10 minutes reading or journaling

- A short session of clarity-oriented work to reconnect inner sense

Also, do not react to others – buffer around them instead.

What most of us don't get is that we typically don't rise to our goals.... *we sink to our environment.* As such, you need to choose those with whom you associate with the same way you choose your tools: *with conscious intention, and with attention.*

With this covered, it is important that you build on what you've picked up here by understanding that progress isn't always about doing more – it really is about cutting off what quietly keeps us from forward motion. You don't need more strategies or more motivation if the issue is that there's something siphoning fuel out of you. You just need to cut the noise and drop the needless burden. Progress accelerates not just by action, but by what you choose to stop allowing as well.

With the hidden drains cleared, it's now time to reverse the idea: to use *friction intentionally.* For example, make distractions harder to access, or make bad habits annoying, etc. This flips productivity *from willpower-based to environment-based.* The next chapter gets into this, in some depth.

CHAPTER 22

USE FRICTION... ON PURPOSE

We're told to do everything we can to eliminate friction – to do everything possible to make everything flow as smoothly and seamlessly as possible, if we are to optimize progress. However, just like bacteria, not all friction is bad. The right kind, in the right place, is an undeniable net positive that can deter your impulses, refine your focus, and support effective follow-through. This chapter explores building positive resistance, so your environment leads you toward what matters, *and not necessarily what's easy.*

Let's get started.

I: Add Friction to the Behaviors You Want to Do Less

When we think about productivity, we tend to think along the lines of making good habits easier to get into and ingrain. However, there's a lesser-known (and lesser-appreciated) strategy for avoiding procrastination that works just as well, if not better: *making bad behaviors more difficult to indulge in.*

This is inhibitory friction – *deliberately inserting small speed bumps between you and your worst impulse behaviors.*

This strategy is not your go-to because you're weak, lack willpower or cannot commit to good habits off the bat... it's your go-to because *design outperforms discipline* nine times out of ten.

See, procrastination often lurks in those habits that are typically too easy to indulge in: scrolling, snacking, tab-switching, inbox-refreshing, et al. You don't choose them... you fall into them. The goal here is to make falling into these habits harder.

Step 1: Determine Your "Impulse Sinkholes"

Think about your most typical go-to escape hatches when you procrastinate:

- What do you normally do when you're "just checking" something?

- What app or habit you tend to get into by accident most?

- What persistent low-effort reward is continually undermining high-effort objectives?

Note down 2-3 habits quietly consuming your time and energy.

Step 2: Add Friction Between You and the Behavior

Now, make each one of these slightly harder to access:

- Digital distractions:
  - Log off of social media websites each day.
  - Delete apps from your home screen on your phone.
  - Set your browser to open on a focus dashboard, and not YouTube or Gmail.

- Physical distractions:
  - Place snacks, phones, or remote controls in another room.
  - Unplug your TV or monitor before bed.
  - Place your gaming controller or Kindle in a locked drawer or container.

- Tempting tools:
  - Use slow apps or two-factor logins for indulgent activities.
  - Turn on grayscale mode or focus blockers during work hours.

Think of these measures as *pause buttons*; as small interruptions that break the trance and give your better judgment time to speak up and assert itself.

Step 3: Use the Pause

When the friction arises, don't rush through it. Ask:

"Is this what I really want to be doing right now?"

Every so often, a 5-second time-out is all it takes to shake yourself loose from autopilot mode, and back to progress.

II: Add Friction to the Start — to Increase Intention

We're often told to ensure that the good habits we pick up and work to ingrain into our psyches are typically established in as swift and frictionless a manner as possible. However, not all tasks benefit from a quick start. *And this is especially true for the ones that truly matter*.

When a task is creative, strategic, or emotionally loaded, starting too fast can lead to shallow work, aimless effort, or premature procrastination. This is where purposeful starting friction comes in.

Your goal here isn't to throw in speed bumps for the sole purpose of causing delays. The purpose here is to prime your mind so that it is better prepared for *focused*, *intentional* effort.

Step 1: Choose a "Start Cue" That Purposely Slows You Down

Make this cue 30-60 seconds long... just enough time to execute a mental gear shift.

Examples:

- Prior to coding: Write down one sentence on the feature or function you are building and why it matters.

- Prior to drafting your client pitch: Paraphrase your main message or the feeling you want the client to take away.

- Before a sales call: Get a quick recall of the prospective client's main pain point and how you will solve it.

This small break graduates you from a mere task-doer to a purpose-driven operator.

Step 2: Introduce a Mini "Clarity Gate" Before Work

Add a checkpoint that forces a moment of clarity and concentration right before action.

Try:

- *A sticky note ritual: "What outcome would make this session worthwhile?"*

- *A voice prompt: "Why in the world do I have to complete this task, now?"*

- *A line for a quick journal entry. "If I only get one thing right, it should be..."*

This removes the possibility of flailing, floundering, or even outright quitting early from confusion and a lack of clarity.

Step 3: Permit Friction Train Concentration

This friction is not resistance… it's investment.

It creates a mental hurdle that says, "This absolutely counts, so you need to listen up and pay attention."

As someone prone to procrastination and delays, that shift from autopilot to attention is the difference between coasting on tasks and working with direction.

As such, it's important not to rush the start. Rather, you need to design it first, so that your work is able to "begin itself" – not from speed, *but from significance.*

III: Use Friction to Protect Your Time

Oftentimes, procrastination has everything to do with "invasion" – your time being pulled apart by emails, messages, random meetings, and interruptions. If everything and everyone has unlimited access to you, your focus gets spread thin and scattered before you've even begun.

That's where access friction becomes your shield. We're not necessarily talking about being unavailable... we're talking about *being intentionally available*. Used well, friction is a time-saving barrier. Think of it not as a wall, but rather as a gate with a lock that you control.

Step 1: Create "Permission Windows" for Distractions

Instead of checking email, social media, or messages on impulse, create small windows where such distractions are allowed.

Examples:

- 11:30–11:45 AM → Email check

- 4:00–4:15 PM → Social scroll + replies

Outside those windows, block the apps, log off, or disable notifications. This friction makes the automatic check feel just inconvenient enough to skip.

Step 2: Protect Deep Work with an "Invite-Only" Calendar

During your focus intervals, set your calendar status as "busy" or "do not disturb." Use scheduling tools (e.g., Calendly[iv] or Google

Calendar^v) to prevent meetings from being booked during those hours unless you explicitly allow it.

Make it absolutely clear, both to yourself and your colleagues: Deep work time is not drop-in time. Speaking of colleagues…

Step 3: Set Access Windows for Others (and Yourself)

Let people you work with, such as colleagues, clients, or collaborators, know your default communication windows. For instance:

- *"Available to receive calls between 2-4 PM weekdays."*
- *"Slack answers replied to by end of day."*

This establishes regular rhythms and removes the stress of 24/7 responsiveness, which is one of the biggest procrastination triggers.

IV: Use Friction to Slow Down Overcommitment

As we highlighted before, one of the sneakiest, yet biggest, causes of procrastination is overcommitment. When your to-do list is too filled with "yeses" you didn't actually mean – or never had time for in the first place – it becomes difficult to accomplish much. Tasks proliferate, focus fails, and motivation ultimately plummets.

The fix for this one, is decision friction: putting intentional pause points in, before you commit to anything new. This slows down impulse-agreements and protects your future bandwidth.

Step 1: Add a "Never Say Yes on the Spot" Rule

Implement a 12-24-hour buffer for all new promises, big and small. Use the phrases:

- *"Let me check my bandwidth and get back to you tomorrow."*

- *"I'd like to think that through. Can I confirm by this evening?"*

This small delay makes enough room between reaction and reflection, and gives you sufficient time to decide if the task is actually possible or just an instant positive.

Step 2: Use a Simple Criteria Checklist Before Agreeing

Before you say yes to a new favor, gig, or project, ask yourself:

- Is it quite in the order of my current priorities?

- Can I honestly commit the time and energy required?

- Will I be sorry/resentful about this activity in the future?

If it fails on *even just one* of these criteria – do not take it on or attempt to re-negotiate its terms. Writing these down as a template keeps the fog and gunk of in-the-moment duress out.

Step 3: Set a Weekly "Capacity Cap"

Establish a soft boundary for new commitments each week (e.g., no more than 2 new outside projects or 5 hours of add-on work). When it's full, everything else gets delayed or rejected... with no guilt whatsoever.

V: Add Friction Between Impulse and Action

Procrastination has a way of hijacking you in the moment – not through big choices, but through small, unnoticed impulses:

- *"Let me just take a look at that message..."*

- *"I just need to Google this one thing..."*
- *"What if I pursued that new idea right now instead?"*

These micro-distractions often add up to hours lost, and the way out of these is via *strategic interruption*. When you create a barrier of friction between impulse and action, you provide your mind with a *chance to choose instead of react*.

Step 1: Install a 10-Second Pause Habit

Before launching into any distracting program or task-switching, wait 10 seconds. Breathe. Ask yourself:

- *"Do I truly want to do this, or is it just an escape?"*
- *"Is now really the best time?"*

This small pause delays gratification long enough for awareness to arise. For an extra kick, place a sticky note on your computer or phone:

"*Pause: What's pulling me?*"

Step 2: Create a "Not Now" List

When something new, something you need to make a detour to do, or a curiosity arises mid-focus, don't go after it immediately... record it first.

Have a small "Not Now" list open beside your work. Jot it down and return to the task.

This keeps your brain from clinging to new ideas, all while guaranteeing that it won't forget either.

Step 3: Use the 20-Minute Rule for Instant Cravings

When you're tempted by distraction, tell yourself, "If I still want to do this in 20 minutes, I can."

Set a timer. Most of our instant wants tend to fade once the window of impulse closes, without having to exercise discipline.

VI: Use Micro-Discomfort to Stay Awake at the Wheel

Procrastination doesn't always start with distraction... at times, it actually starts with lethargy. By lethargy, we mean the mental droop where your energy dips, and "I'll get going in five minutes" becomes "maybe tomorrow." The answer to lethargy, is incorporating mild, voluntary discomfort that keeps you mentally alert and on target.

Micro-discomfort isn't pain, either. Think of it as gentle, beneficial tension – enough to keep you alert at the wheel of your own attention.

Step 1: Shift to a Slightly Uncomfortable Position

When you find yourself zoning out, change your physical state:

- Stand up at a standing desk or countertop.

- Sit on a stool instead of a comfy couch.

- Work in an alternate room that doesn't have a couch.

The idea here is to wake up your brain... to tell it: "We're shifting now." And a lot of the time, you'll realize that this mild discomfort is just what the doctor ordered to get back on track mentally.

Step 2: Use a Visible Timer to Trigger Healthy Pressure

Time abundance often fosters procrastination. Fix this by making your time concrete and limited:

- Set a 15-30-minute timer on your workspace.

- Use a sand timer, kitchen timer, or visual countdown software.

This activates low-level urgency without fear. It transforms aimless effort into a disciplined sprint, in so doing enlivening the aspect of your brain that responds to challenge.

Step 3: Say Your Task Aloud Before You Start

Before you start, clearly and firmly say:

- *"I'm going to outline the first three slides."*

- *"This block is for unpacking every new item and stacking everything onto respective shelves."*

This vocal cue *adds deliberate intention to your effort*, which closes the mental gap between thinking about a task and actually getting started on it.

Friction isn't the problem, a lot of the time... *unintentional* friction is. When used wisely, resistance becomes one of the most valuable allies you can have. It guards your focus, strengthens your choices, and aligns your environment with your goals. It makes the right actions easier to kick off, and the wrong ones harder to slip into.

CONCLUSION

You made it.

You've shifted from *cracking the code on procrastination...* to *rewiring your thinking, feeling, and acting...* to *building momentum that you can actually sustain.*

You're here now: not "fixed," not perfect – but attuned, armed, and alert. And that's most definitely not a small thing. In fact, *it's everything.*

As you've most certainly picked up by now, this book wasn't about becoming some flawlessly optimized productivity machine. It was about this:

- Understanding why you procrastinate (and doing so without judgment).

- Seeing how you can change (without pretending it's easy).

- And developing habits, mindsets, and systems that serve you (even when life/conditions/environment is less than ideal).

And that's how *real progress* in the real, unidealized world almost always happens.

Not all at once, and most certainly not just when you feel like it.

But because you've decided to show up, and you've decided to do so with intention.

So, keep this in mind, regardless of whatever position/situation/age-range you are in:

You are not behind.
You're not too late.
You're not broken.
You're alive and ready.

And that's what matters the most.

Closing Challenge: Pick One Change. *Do It Now.*

Before you put this book down, don't attempt to do everything. Don't aim for the whole set of skittles to fell, now that you're armed with the complete know-how package.

Just pick one thing, and act on it today, and then so the same tomorrow, and so forth.

Perhaps you:

- Start your "Good Enough" task log

- Book an hour for deep work next week (and defend it)

- Write a quick "action protocol" for a task type that you regularly procrastinate

- Sketch your "non-comparative dashboard" and pin it where you'll see it

- Enact your first friction rule: remove one drain, or introduce one delay

Etc.

One shift. One step. One start.

That's all.

Because the only method for defeating procrastination is the same method by which you defeat fear, haze, and uncertainty:

By moving forward just once. And then rinsing and repeating the same.

Final Note: Make This Your Personalized Living System

This is not the kind of book to read and just set aside.

This is a book to keep near at all times, and to promptly return to when things (inevitably) start to slide once more.

You'll get stuck and you'll most likely get lost too. That's human.

But now you know how to get back.

You know how to reboot without shame, rewire intentionally, and keep moving forward. And you know how to do it efficiently... not through brute force, but through repeated practice.

I repeat again...

You don't need to feel ready.

You don't even need to execute every lesson we've outlined here perfectly (or even properly.)

You just need to try your level best.

That is all.

Now go.

---

[i] https://medium.com/clear-yo-mind/emotional-regulation-the-simple-neuroscience-behind-name-it-to-tame-it-b22924bb543d
[ii] https://www.focusmate.com/
[iii] https://flown.com/home?t=msg&expSkip=true
[iv] https://calendly.com/
[v] https://calendar.google.com/calendar/u/0/r?pli=1